# COMMONSENSE AND OUTCOME-DRIVEN MARKETING FOR AUTHORS

## PROVEN STRATEGIES TO BOOST BOOK SALES AND ACHIEVE PUBLISHING SUCCESS WITHOUT BREAKING THE BANK

### STEPHANIE KROL, Ed.D.

RILEY
Publishing

Commonsense and Outcome-Driven Marketing for Authors: Proven Strategies to Boost Book Sales and Achieve Publishing Success without Breaking the Bank

Published by Riley Publishing Wheaton, IL

Copyright ©2025 Stephanie Krol, Ed.D. All rights reserved.

No part of this book may be reproduced in any form or by any mechanical means, including information storage and retrieval systems, without permission in writing from the publisher/author, except by a reviewer who may quote passages in a review.

All images, logos, quotes, and trademarks included in this book are subject to use according to trademark and copyright laws of the United States of America.

Names: Krol, Stephanie, author.

Title: Commonsense and outcome-driven marketing for authors: proven strategies to boost book sales and achieve publishing success without breaking the bank / Stephanie Krol, Ed.D.

Description: Wheaton, IL : Riley Publishing, [2025] | Includes bibliographical references.

Identifiers: ISBN: 9781737320128 (paperback) | 9781737320166 (spiral-bound paperback) | 9781737320142 (hardcover) | 9781737320159 (Ebook)

Subjects: LCSH: Books--Marketing. | Selling--Books. | Internet marketing. | Booksellers and bookselling. | Publishers and publishing. | Book industries and trade. | BISAC: LANGUAGE ARTS & DISCIPLINES / Writing / Business Aspects. | BUSINESS & ECONOMICS / Marketing / General. | BUSINESS & ECONOMICS / E-Commerce / Digital Marketing.

Classification: LCC: Z285.6 .K76 2025 | DDC: 070.5029--dc23

Copyright owned by Stephanie Krol, Ed.D.

All rights reserved by Stephanie Krol, Ed.D., and Riley Publishing.

Book Cover Design and Interior Formatting by 100Covers.

Printed in the United States of America.

Paperback ISBN - 978-1-7373201-2-8
Hardback ISBN - 978-1-7373201-4-2
Ebook ISBN - 978-1-7373201-5-9

# CONTENTS

Preface . . . . . . . . . . . . . . . . . . . . . . . . . . . . . . . . . . . . . . . . vii
Acknowledgments . . . . . . . . . . . . . . . . . . . . . . . . . . . . . . . ix
Introduction . . . . . . . . . . . . . . . . . . . . . . . . . . . . . . . . . . . . xi

Chapter 1: Laying the Foundation . . . . . . . . . . . . . . . . . . 1
Chapter 2: Building Your Brand . . . . . . . . . . . . . . . . . . . 11
Chapter 3: Creating Your Online Platform . . . . . . . . . . . . 21
Chapter 4: Engaging Your Audience Early . . . . . . . . . . . . 35
Chapter 5: Preparing for Launch . . . . . . . . . . . . . . . . . . 49
Chapter 6: Gaining Credibility and Reviews . . . . . . . . . . 57
Chapter 7: The Three-Week Social Media Rollout Plan . . . 67
Chapter 8: Launching Your Book . . . . . . . . . . . . . . . . . . 71
Chapter 9: Your Book Is Live—Now What? . . . . . . . . . . . 85
Chapter 10: Leveraging Reviews and Community Support . . . . . . 99
Chapter 11: Marketing Your Book . . . . . . . . . . . . . . . . . 113
Chapter 12: Sustaining Momentum . . . . . . . . . . . . . . . . 125
Chapter 13: Bonus: Wrap-Up Chapter: Bringing It All Together . . 143
Chapter 14: Bonus: How to Avoid a Bad Publishing Experience . . 149
Chapter 15: Bonus: Top Twenty-Five Paths to Success for
    Goal-Driven Authors . . . . . . . . . . . . . . . . . . . . . . 159
Chapter 16: Tools and Templates for Authors . . . . . . . . . . 183

Appendix . . . . . . . . . . . . . . . . . . . . . . . . . . . . . . . . . . . 197
References . . . . . . . . . . . . . . . . . . . . . . . . . . . . . . . . . 211
Your Feedback Means the World to Me . . . . . . . . . . . . . . 215
About the Author . . . . . . . . . . . . . . . . . . . . . . . . . . . . 217
Invite Dr. Stephanie to Speak at Your Next Event . . . . . . . 221

This book is dedicated to my incredible author clients, whose relentless drive to do more, learn more, and build more inspires me every day. Your passion motivates me to grow, refine, and continually strive to provide the resources and options you deserve. Thank you for trusting me with your journeys—your success is my greatest reward.

I also dedicate this book to my mom, whose unwavering belief in me has been my compass. Her words, "You can do it," have been a constant reminder of my potential. She has never placed limits on what I can achieve, and her love, support, and presence ground me, keeping me resilient and moving forward. Mom, you are my rock and my cheerleader. I am so grateful.

# PREFACE

When I first entered the world of publishing, I quickly realized that writing a book was only half the battle. The other half? Picking the correct type of publishing for me, then ensuring it found its way into the hands of readers. Like many authors, I assumed that simply creating a great book would be enough. But as I soon discovered, even the most brilliant stories can get lost without a clear marketing strategy.

This realization wasn't just humbling—it was the catalyst for my journey into the world of book marketing. Over the years, I've helped authors navigate the often-confusing waters of promoting their books. In doing so, I've learned that success doesn't come from expensive, overhyped solutions. It comes from practical, goal-oriented strategies tailored to each author's unique vision.

This book is a culmination of everything I've learned. It's the guide I wish I'd had when I first started—direct, actionable, filled with examples to follow, and designed with your success in mind. My hope is that it empowers you to confidently market your book, connect with your readers, and achieve the goals you've worked so hard to reach.

To every author who has poured their heart and soul into their work and needed direction, examples, and actionable steps: this book is for you.

# ACKNOWLEDGMENTS

This book would not have been possible without the incredible support and collaboration of so many along the way.

To the authors I've had the privilege of working with—thank you for allowing me to be part of your journeys. Your creativity and resilience continue to inspire me, and I'm honored to help bring your work to life.

To my team at Riley-Infinity—your dedication and professionalism make everything we do possible. You ensure that every author has the resources and support they need to succeed, and I am endlessly grateful for your hard work.

To my family, friends, and mentors—thank you for your encouragement, wisdom, and belief in me. Your unwavering support has made this journey not only possible but meaningful.

Finally, to my readers—thank you for trusting me to guide you through this process. This book is for you, and I can't wait to see the incredible impact you'll make as you share your book with the world.

# INTRODUCTION

Congratulations! You've done the hard part—you've written your book. As any author knows, this is no small feat. It takes countless hours of dedication, creativity, and focus to bring an idea to life on the page. Take a moment to acknowledge that accomplishment.

But now, a new challenge awaits: getting your book into the hands of readers. That's where this guide comes in. Whether you're a first-time author or a seasoned writer, activating a marketing plan is crucial to your book's success.

## The Common Struggle

Many authors find marketing to be a daunting task. You may have heard phrases like, "You need a marketing plan," but when it comes to the "how," the guidance is often lacking or misleading. Overpromising marketing services can leave you frustrated and with little to show for your investment.

I've been there. When I launched my book, I encountered the same confusion and overwhelm. Over time, through trial and error, I developed a marketing approach that works. It's this plan that I now share with you to make your journey easier.

## What This Book Is About

This is not just another guide filled with vague advice and lofty promises. This book offers a practical, step-by-step marketing plan tailored for authors who want results. It's designed to be both actionable and efficient, avoiding unnecessary fluff. Every step is geared toward helping you market your book effectively, whether you're aiming for local success, online sales, or building your brand as an author.

## How to Use This Plan

Think of this as your roadmap. It covers everything from prelaunch marketing to long-term strategies for maintaining momentum after your book is published. You'll find simple, effective tips that have been refined over years of practice.

While every marketing strategy should be customized to fit your unique situation—your book, your audience, and your goals—this plan gives you a comprehensive framework to build upon.

## Structure of the Book

This book is divided into ten main sections, each covering a key phase of your book's marketing journey:

- **Laying the Foundation**
  Defining your target reader and setting up essential elements like your domain and publishing name.

- **Building Your Brand**
  Craft concise bios, set up Google Alerts, and establish a professional presence.

- **Creating Your Online Platform**
  Develop your website, set up payment systems, and create lead magnets.

- **Engaging Your Audience Early**
  Use social media and PR tools to increase visibility.

- **Preparing for Launch**
  Create book trailers, optimize back matter, and utilize PR opportunities.

- **Gaining Credibility and Reviews**
  Submit for trade reviews and build excitement prelaunch.

- **Launching Your Book**
  Plan a launch event and optimize online visibility.
- **Expanding Your Reach**
  Organize virtual tours and use podcasts to widen your audience.
- **Leveraging Reviews and Community Support**
  Focus on gathering reviews and collaborating with community groups.
- **Sustaining Momentum**
  Keep marketing alive with contests and outreach to libraries. Continue refining strategies for future releases.

At the end, you'll find best practices for continuing your marketing efforts long after the initial honeymoon period. There's also a timeline to help you visualize the process.

Whether you're starting before your book's launch or even after, it's never too late to implement a smart, focused marketing strategy. This book will serve as your guide to reaching your readers and growing your presence as an author.

Let's get started!

# CHAPTER 1

## LAYING THE FOUNDATION

In the ever-evolving world of book marketing, success doesn't happen by accident. It requires intention, strategy, and a strong foundation. For many authors, the journey to a successful launch can feel like walking a tightrope—balancing writing, publishing, and promotion while managing the overwhelm of where to start. That's where *Riley-Infinity* steps in.

Riley-Infinity emerged from a deep understanding of these challenges—a collective of marketing strategists, publishing experts, and creative professionals who recognized the unique struggles authors face in an increasingly competitive literary marketplace. We aren't just another publishing services company or our partner digital marketing company; we're strategic partners dedicated to translating an author's creative vision into a compelling narrative that resonates with readers and industry professionals alike, and we don't create just another book, we endeavor to make each book custom, special, and a work of art from the front of the cover to the back. We take pride in doing our best to create your work of art, and like our tagline says, "Your choice for quality and service with a dash of Infinitude!"

The publishing ecosystem has dramatically transformed in recent years. Traditional pathways have been disrupted by digital platforms, social media marketing, and increasingly sophisticated reader engagement strategies. Authors no longer simply write books; they must become brands, storytellers, and strategic communicators. This multifaceted landscape demands expertise that extends far beyond writing exceptional prose.

Our approach at Riley-Infinity is systematically comprehensive, breaking down the book marketing process into strategic, manageable phases. We begin with a deep-dive discovery session, where we explore not just the book's content but also the author's unique voice, target audience, and strategic objectives, all while leaving the meeting knowing your cost and items listed in your customized proposal. This initial consultation allows us to develop a customized roadmap that aligns with the author's specific goals and the book's inherent strengths.

At *Riley-Infinity*, we are dedicated to supporting authors at every stage of their journey. We specialize in turning ambitious book ideas into actionable plans for success. Whether you're overwhelmed by the logistics of marketing or just unsure of the next steps in your self-publishing process, our process ensures nothing slips through the cracks and that your book process is not overwhelming and keeps the momentum throughout until your book is up worldwide. We're here to help you lay the strongest possible foundation for your book's success—step by step, efficiently, and with the utmost care.

## Let's Dive In, Starting at the Beginning: Defining Your Target Reader Avatar

The first step in your book marketing journey is identifying your *ideal reader*—a detailed, specific portrait of who you're writing for. This is often referred to as creating a *target reader avatar*. Why does this matter? Because when you speak to everyone, you speak to no one. Targeting allows your message to land with impact. Your avatar becomes the guiding force behind every email, post, or promotional campaign you create.

Start by asking yourself key questions to narrow down your audience:

- **Who are they?** (Are they middle-aged professionals, retirees, or young entrepreneurs?)
- **What is their demographic?** Age, gender, occupation, education, and location.
- **What are their interests, pain points, and desires?** Do they crave personal growth? Are they looking for a gripping escape in fiction, or do they turn to books to solve a specific problem?
- **What motivates them to pick up a book?** Relaxation, professional knowledge, emotional connection?

Let's say your audience is men aged forty to seventy who work in corporate settings or national industries. These readers might value leadership, history, self-improvement, or gripping nonfiction that speaks to their personal and professional lives. If this is your audience, every marketing element—tone, imagery, content—should be tailored to their values and interests.

For this example, when crafting promotional material:

- Choose *clean, authoritative designs* over flashy or colorful layouts.
- Use *language that aligns with their professional mindset*: concise, direct, and insightful.
- Highlight the value your book brings: lessons, inspiration, or new perspectives they can apply.

At Riley-Infinity, this process is streamlined. Together, we'll define your audience in a targeted, data-backed way. We identify key traits, habits, and motivations, ensuring your avatar isn't based on guesswork but grounded in strategy. Many people miss this step altogether or think they have done it, and it is not deep or rich enough. Without this step taken properly, everything beyond it will not be nearly as effective. From there, your book's messaging is clear, consistent, and connects deeply with readers.

## Securing Key Elements: Domains, Publishing Company Name, and Author Name

With your audience defined, the next foundational step is building your *online presence*. Your website and domain act as a virtual storefront—one that readers, media, and industry contacts will visit repeatedly. Securing your domains early prevents confusion and ensures a professional, credible launch.

1. **Author Domain:** Your name should take center stage. Whether you're releasing one book or planning an entire series, owning a clean, memorable domain like *your-name.com* is critical. Avoid unnecessary symbols or creative spellings—stick to professional, searchable options. Platforms like *GoDaddy* and *Cloudflare* make purchasing domains simple and affordable.

2. **Publishing Company Name:** If you're self-publishing, create a professional publishing imprint. Even if it's just for your books, it adds credibility and trust to your brand. Think of names that reflect your values, genre, or long-term goals. Examples might include *Steel River Press* for thrillers or *Legacy Path Publishing* for memoirs.

3. **Book-Specific Domains:** Securing domains for your book title (and variations) is equally important. Readers often type book titles directly into search engines—owning the domain guarantees they'll land on your website rather than getting lost in unrelated search results.

**Pro Tip:** Redirect all your domains (author, publishing company, and book) to one central hub—your author website. A clean, easy-to-navigate site builds trust and gives readers a clear path to explore your work, sign up for newsletters, or make purchases.

At *Riley-Infinity*, we manage this entire process with you utilizing your input throughout, while keeping your book moving forward and on task. We research availability, secure domains, and ensure your online presence aligns perfectly with your brand. You focus on your book; we'll make sure readers can find it.

## Researching Critical Marketing Elements: Best Keywords and Hashtags

Once you've defined your target reader, the next step in building a solid marketing foundation is researching keywords and hashtags to connect with them effectively. We understand that this step can be time-consuming and overwhelming for authors juggling multiple responsibilities. That's why we offer expert keyword research as part of our marketing plans, ensuring you get the visibility your book deserves.

**Why Keywords Matter:**

Keywords are the backbone of online discoverability. They serve as the bridge between your book and the readers actively searching for it—whether on Amazon, Google, or social media platforms. A well-researched keyword strategy ensures your book reaches the right people at the right time, boosting sales and expanding your audience.

Start by compiling a list of your top twenty keywords. These should include terms related to your book's:

- **Genre** (e.g., "historical romance," "psychological thriller")
- **Themes** (e.g., "redemption story," "overcoming trauma")
- **Setting** (e.g., "Victorian London," "rural Appalachia")
- **Character Types** (e.g., "strong female lead," "anti-hero protagonist")

Don't stop at single words—think bigger with *longtail keywords*. These are phrases of three to five words that reflect specific search terms readers use, such as:

- "Coming-of-age novel in rural America"
- "Corporate exit strategies for professionals"
- "Strong female detective mystery series"

Longtail keywords are particularly powerful because they have less competition but high intent. Readers typing these phrases already know what they're looking for, which makes them more likely to buy.

Tools to Simplify Keyword Research

We use proven tools like Keywords Everywhere, Publisher Rocket, and Amazon's auto-fill feature to uncover the most relevant, high-performing keywords in your genre. For authors working independently, these tools can help streamline your research:

1. **Keywords Everywhere:** A browser extension that displays search volume, cost-per-click (CPC), and competition data for keywords as you browse Google, Amazon, or YouTube.
2. **Publisher Rocket:** Specifically designed for authors, it identifies highly searched, low-competition keywords to optimize your Amazon listings.
3. **Amazon Auto-Fill:** Start typing a keyword into Amazon's search bar and pay attention to the suggestions. These auto-filled phrases reflect real search trends from readers.

**How We Help:** At *Riley-Infinity*, we do the digging for you. Whether your book focuses on corporate transitions like "dismissed from job," "corporate exit," or "hostile takeovers," or explores fiction themes like "grief recovery" or "strong female leads," we pinpoint keywords that align with your book and audience. By our next call, we'll deliver a refined keyword list tailored to boost your visibility and attract your ideal readers.

### Strategic Keyword Placement

Researching the right keywords is just the first step. The next step is integrating them seamlessly across your marketing materials. Keywords should appear naturally, not forced, to avoid harming your search engine ranking—a common issue known as *keyword stuffing*.

Here's where to incorporate keywords:

- **Your book description**: Craft a compelling description that includes key phrases while remaining engaging and natural.
- **Author bio**: Highlight relevant keywords that establish your expertise or align with your audience's interests.
- **Blog posts and articles**: Use keywords in headlines, subheadings, and body content to attract search engine traffic.
- **Social media captions**: Sprinkle keywords into your posts, ensuring your content remains relatable and authentic.

For example, if your book explores themes of corporate job loss, a sample caption might read: *"Laid off. Dismissed. Pushed out. The words change, but the pain is the same. My new book shares stories of resilience and rebuilding after the corporate exit no one plans for."*

### Maximizing Hashtag Reach

While keywords help readers find you on search engines, hashtags are essential for discoverability on platforms like **Instagram**, **X (formerly Twitter)**, and **TikTok**. Readers frequently use hashtags to find books within their favorite genres, follow trending topics, and engage with authors.

## Creating a Hashtag List

We recommend creating a master list of hashtags organized by categories, such as:

1. **Genre-Specific:**
   #HistoricalFiction #RomanticThriller #LitFic
2. **Reader Community:**
   #BookTok #Bookstagram #AmReading #IndieAuthors
3. **Themes and Topics:**
   #RedemptionStory #StrongFemaleLead #CorporateHarassment
4. **Trends and Events:**
   #NewBookRelease #WritersLife #MondayMotivation

To find the most effective hashtags:

- Use tools like **Hashtagify.me** and **Twitag** to analyze the popularity and relevance of hashtags in your niche.
- Research successful authors in your genre and take note of the hashtags they use consistently.
- Test different combinations of hashtags to see which generates the most engagement.

## Consistency Is Key

Keep your list of top-performing hashtags at your desk or in a digital note file for quick access. Incorporate them naturally into your posts, alternating between broad and niche hashtags. For example, a post promoting a coming-of-age novel might include:

- Broad: #BookLovers #NewNovel #ComingOfAge
- Niche: #RuralFiction #RedemptionJourney #SmallTownStories

Our team streamlines this process for authors. We research, curate, and refine a customized hashtag strategy designed to amplify your content's reach while keeping it relevant to your audience.

## Research is Key: Research Successful Leaders who are Authors in your Genre

One of the most effective ways to develop your marketing strategy is by studying authors who have already mastered the game in your genre. These authors offer a roadmap of proven tactics that you can adapt to fit your unique voice and audience.

**How to Research Genre Leaders**

Here's how you can do it step by step:

1. **Identify Key Authors:** Start with a Google search or browse Amazon for bestselling books in your genre. Look for authors with large followings, positive reviews, and consistent engagement.
2. **Analyze Their Content:** Visit their websites and social media platforms. Take note of:
   - **Content Types:** Are they posting book updates, writing tips, Q&A sessions, or behind-the-scenes glimpses?
   - **Platforms:** Where are they most active—Instagram, Facebook, LinkedIn, or TikTok?
   - **Engagement Style:** How do they interact with readers? What tone do they use—friendly, professional, or humorous?
3. **Break Down Their Strategy:** Pay attention to their:
   - Hashtag usage
   - Keyword placement in book descriptions and posts
   - Email newsletters and how they connect with readers beyond social media

4. **Reverse-Engineer What Works**: Once you've studied their strategy, adapt what resonates with your brand. For instance:
    - If you admire an author's weekly "behind-the-scenes" videos, create your version to share insights about your writing process.
    - If they leverage niche hashtags to gain visibility, test similar hashtags that align with your book's themes.

## How Riley-Infinity Helps

For authors who find this process daunting, Riley-Infinity steps in. We can take note of your genre, unravel a marketing plan, that identifies actionable strategies that you can implement. From finding keyword-rich book descriptions to curating an inspired content calendar, we streamline every step, so you can focus on your writing.

By understanding what makes your genre's leaders successful—and combining it with your unique voice—you can carve out your place in the literary landscape and build a dedicated readership.

# CHAPTER 2

## BUILDING YOUR BRAND

The moment you begin promoting yourself as an author, every detail matters. Your author brand isn't just about flashy marketing—it's the **identity readers attach to your name.** It represents the promise of what they'll find when they open your books, visit your website, or engage with your social media content. Think of it as the unique combination of your voice, personality, and the themes that define your work. Building a strong brand allows you to stand out in a crowded marketplace, attract the right readers, and leave a lasting impression.

Every aspect of your professional presence—from your bio and website to the tone of your social media posts—feeds into this larger identity. Your brand isn't just what you say about yourself; it's how others perceive you based on the stories you tell, the values you represent, and the experiences you share. Readers aren't just buying your books; they're buying into **you** as an author, storyteller, and creator. By being intentional about how you present yourself, you create a sense of consistency and trust that resonates across platforms.

At its core, your author brand is about authenticity. Flashy marketing strategies may grab attention briefly, but readers connect with authors who are genuine and relatable. Your brand should reflect your unique voice and values, whether you're writing thrillers that keep readers on edge or heartfelt memoirs that inspire reflection. Consider the emotions you want your readers to associate with your name: Are you the writer who challenges their worldview, makes them laugh, or helps them escape into a new reality? Aligning all your promotional materials—your bio, visuals, newsletters, and tone—with this identity ensures that readers know exactly what to expect. Furthermore, an author brand is a long-term investment. It grows with you as a writer, evolving with every book you publish and every interaction you have with your audience. Building this brand requires patience and consistency, but its rewards are immense.

To start, one of the simplest yet most effective tools is your **author bio**. Crafting a concise, impactful bio is essential for establishing your voice and authority. Equally important is setting up a **professional email signature** that subtly promotes your book with every message you send.

## Write Concise Author Bios

Crafting concise, professional author bios is a key step in building your brand and credibility as an author. A well-written bio introduces you to your audience, establishes your expertise, and encourages readers to connect with your work. To ensure versatility, you'll need two versions of your bio: a thirty-five-word version and a seventy-five-word version. Each serves a specific purpose, and together, they ensure your brand message remains consistent across platforms.

### Thirty-Five-Word Bio

The thirty-five-word bio is your elevator pitch—it's short, sharp, and focused. It's ideal for bylines, email signatures, and quick introductions where space is limited. This version highlights your core credentials, book title, and the value you bring as an author.

**Example:** *"Stephanie Krol, a best-selling author and founder of Riley-Infinity, empowers authors with over a decade of experience. She specializes in books that inspire growth, influence, and legacy, guiding authors toward publishing success."*

This version works well because it's **direct, keyword-focused,** and easy for readers to digest at a glance. We support authors by helping refine these short bios, ensuring they convey the right tone and highlight your most impactful achievements.

Seventy-Five-Word Bio

The seventy-five-word bio expands on your background and offers more context about your work. It's ideal for **websites, book promotions, speaking engagements,** and press kits. This version provides a broader snapshot of your experience, notable achievements, and the themes or genres you specialize in. Be sure to incorporate relevant keywords that align with your brand and genre to optimize for discoverability. **Example:** *"Stephanie Krol is a best-selling author and the founder of Riley-Infinity. With over a decade of experience, she has helped countless authors navigate the writing and publishing journey. Stephanie specializes in creating books that inspire growth, build influence, and leave lasting legacies. Her dedication to empowering new authors has shaped her successful career, making her a trusted mentor in the self-publishing world. Stephanie's work continues to transform lives through expertly crafted publications."*

This version is professional, engaging, and versatile—it gives readers a deeper understanding of who you are and why they should trust your work.

Bios are drafted, refined, and tailored for specific platforms to ensure your professional image remains cohesive and polished. Need help? Send your drafted bios to Stephanie for final polishing to make sure they resonate with your audience.

## Set Up Google Alerts

Once your bios are in place, the next step in monitoring and managing your brand is setting up Google Alerts. Staying aware of where your name, book titles, or associated keywords appear online is crucial for growing your presence, engaging with readers, and identifying new opportunities.

**Why Use Google Alerts?**

Google Alerts is a **free tool** that sends you email notifications whenever specific keywords are mentioned online. For authors, this includes your name, book title, and any industry-related terms that align with your brand. By tracking these mentions, you can:

- **Monitor your online reputation**: Stay informed about how your work is being received or discussed.
- **Engage with readers and media**: Quickly respond to reviews, interviews, or reader discussions.
- **Discover marketing opportunities**: Spot articles, book lists, or influencers that align with your genre and brand.

**How to Set Up Google Alerts**

1. **Visit Google Alerts**: Go to google.com/alerts.
2. **Enter Your Keywords**: Start with the basics—your full author name, book title(s), and any relevant terms or phrases connected to your book. Riley-Infinity recommends expanding your list to include keywords like:
    - *"author name," "book title," "best historical fiction of [year]," "book reviews for [book title]."*
    - Niche phrases like *"strong female lead," "thriller with psychological twists,"* or themes like *"corporate job loss"* if applicable.

3. **Set Preferences**: Customize your alerts by selecting:
   - **Sources**: Blogs, news sites, videos, discussions, or all sources.
   - **Frequency**: As-it-happens, daily, or weekly. Choose "daily" for regular updates without being overwhelmed.
   - **Region**: Narrow alerts to specific countries or keep them global.
4. **Refine Over Time**: Regularly update your alerts as your career evolves. Add keywords tied to new book titles, upcoming events, or related trends in your genre.

We ensure you're tracking the right terms—those that will provide insights into your growing influence and allow you to act on opportunities as they arise.

**Keywords to Track**

To maximize the value of Google Alerts, consider tracking the following types of keywords:

- **Your Name and Book Titles**: To catch media mentions, reviews, or reader discussions.
- **Industry-Specific Terms**: *"best self-help books," "top romance novels,"* or *"historical fiction debut authors."*
- **Thematic Keywords**: Keywords related to your book's core themes or plotlines. For example:
  - Corporate-related themes: *"business ethics," "dismissed from job," "hostile corporate takeovers."*
  - Fiction genres: *"thriller with corporate espionage," "small-town mystery series."*
  - Self-help/nonfiction themes: *"scaling influence," "personal growth books."*

By choosing a mix of specific and broad terms, you'll cast a wide enough net to monitor mentions that matter most. Riley-Infinity helps authors develop a **customized keyword strategy** to ensure their Google Alerts deliver meaningful, actionable insights.

### Why It Matters

Staying informed with Google Alerts gives you an edge in an increasingly crowded digital landscape. When you know what's being said about you and your work, you can:

- **Amplify positive mentions**: Share glowing reviews, interviews, or features on your platforms.
- **Address misconceptions or concerns**: Respond to critical feedback professionally to demonstrate engagement.
- **Spot trends in your niche**: Notice how similar books or topics are being discussed, which can inform your marketing strategy.

## Get Professional Headshots That Resonate with Your Brand

Your headshot is often the first visual impression readers, media outlets, or industry professionals have of you, so investing in professional photography is nonnegotiable. Whether it's for your book cover, author website, social media platforms, or press kits, a polished, professional headshot signals credibility and thoughtfulness.

### What Makes a Great Headshot?

A classic head-and-shoulders shot is the foundation for all your branding needs. Think of it as your anchor image—versatile and timeless. Dress in a style that reflects both your personality and your book's theme. For instance, if you're writing business leadership guides, opt for tailored professional attire that conveys authority and confidence. For children's authors, a warm, playful expression with colorful accents might resonate better with your audience.

However, one headshot isn't enough. **Diverse shots offer versatility** for different platforms and campaigns. Consider adding:

1. **Dynamic or Candid Shots:** A shot of you in action—speaking at an event, signing books, or engaged in deep thought—can convey authenticity and storytelling.

2. **Thematic Shots:** Incorporate props or environments tied to your subject matter. Holding your book, sitting in a library, or using subtle elements like corporate backdrops for business books or cozy, natural scenes for memoirs can deepen your visual brand.

3. **Mood and Pose Variety:** Aim for photos that show confident, approachable, and reflective versions of yourself. These nuanced shots provide options for more formal media profiles, informal social media posts, or marketing banners.

From selecting the right photographer to guiding your wardrobe and shot list, our goal is to make this step stress-free and empowering for authors.

**Why It Matters**

Headshots are more than just photos—they're a visual story about who you are as an author. When done right, they help readers and media immediately connect with your message and your book. By having a consistent, professional image across platforms, you'll build trust and recognition, reinforcing your identity every time someone sees you.

## Set Up Your Email Signature Using a Dedicated Service

Your email signature is an underutilized but highly effective marketing tool. Every email you send—whether to friends, clients, or industry contacts—is an opportunity to promote your book and build your brand.

## Why Your Email Signature Matters

Think of your signature as a mini-billboard for your author brand. Even before your book launches, you can begin generating buzz. Something as simple as:

*"Jane Doe, Author of the upcoming [Book Title] | Coming [Month, Year]."*

creates subtle anticipation while reminding people of your upcoming release.

Once your book is available for pre-order or purchase, your signature becomes a direct sales tool:

- Include a **link to your Amazon page** or a dedicated book website.
- Highlight **events** such as upcoming book signings, virtual readings, or launch dates.
- Add **social media icons** to connect with readers and grow your platform.

## How to Set Up a Professional Email Signature

To elevate your signature, use tools like **WiseStamp** or **Newoldstamp**. These platforms allow you to:

1. **Add Branding Elements**: Incorporate your author logo, book cover image, or professional headshot for a sleek, cohesive look.
2. **Include Clickable Links**: Direct readers to your book sales page, social media profiles, or event registrations.
3. **Customize Easily**: Tailor your signature for specific promotions (e.g., pre-order links during launch season) without technical hassle.

**Example of an Effective Email Signature:**

*Jane Doe*
*Award-Winning Author of [Book Title]["Grab your copy here!"] (hyperlinked to Amazon)*
*Follow me: [LinkedIn Icon] [Instagram Icon] [Website Link]*

If you're managing your own setup, **Riley-Infinity** recommends starting with WiseStamp for its user-friendly templates. However, we also offer dedicated support to create, design, and integrate your email signature across Gmail, Outlook, Yahoo, or any other platform.

## Add Sales Links: Simplify Purchasing

To maximize sales opportunities, include easy purchasing options. Services like **Linktree** provide a single page with all your links—perfect for connecting readers to your book, website, and events in one place. Linktree can be included in your email signature to streamline navigation and improve user experience.

Your email signature works silently in the background to promote your book with every interaction. It's professional, unobtrusive, and can reach potential readers without additional effort. Riley-Infinity's authors know the value of this simple strategy because we integrate it into their marketing plans.

Building your author brand requires small, intentional steps that work together to create a professional and engaging presence. By investing in professional headshots, leveraging your email signature for promotion, and setting up direct payment systems, you'll create a foundation for long-term success.

At Riley-Infinity, we partner with you throughout the entire experience, so you are assured your book will get done and up worldwide. We ensure every detail is managed in the publishing services process, outlined right in your proposal, so you can focus on editing, partnering in the process and connecting with readers. Each step we take brings you closer to the successful book launch you've envisioned.

# CHAPTER 3

## CREATING YOUR ONLINE PLATFORM

Creating a strong online platform is key to establishing your presence as an author. This chapter will guide you through the essential steps to set up your digital foundation, starting with the most important tool: your website. Your website will serve as the hub for all your marketing efforts, from selling your book to engaging with your audience.

We'll also cover the creation of payment systems, ensuring you're ready to accept orders seamlessly, and gathering the necessary files for promotions.

### Setting Up Your Payment Gateway

As an author, setting up a reliable payment system is essential for selling your book directly to readers. Today's mobile and online payment tools make it easier than ever to accept payments without the hassle of traditional merchant services.

**Choosing Your Payment System:** To sell your book online or at events, you'll need a system that allows you to take credit card payments securely. The most popular platforms are **Square**, **PayPal**, and **Venmo**. These services are user-friendly, cost nothing to apply for, and have no monthly fees, making them perfect for indie authors.

- **Square:** Ideal for physical sales at events like book signings. You can take payments via card readers or your phone. Square's processing fee is around 2.75 percent per transaction, making it a low-cost solution for authors.
- **PayPal:** A global leader in online payments, PayPal is ideal for selling directly from your website. It offers easy integration with most eCommerce platforms and charges around 2.9 percent plus a fixed fee for each transaction. PayPal also offers invoicing features, which can be handy for bulk orders or business-related sales.
- **Venmo:** A more informal tool for payments, Venmo allows you to accept payments via your mobile app. Venmo is particularly useful for personal sales or smaller transactions but still charges a processing fee similar to PayPal and Square.

**How to Set It Up:** Once you choose your payment system, setting it up is easy. Simply create an account, link it to your bank, and start accepting payments. For each service, you can either manually enter card details, use a card reader, or send an invoice through the platform. Each transaction will come with a small processing fee, but the convenience and security these platforms offer make it well worth the cost.

**Security and Trust:** These platforms are highly secure, offering fraud protection and encryption so your customers can confidently pay for your book without worrying about their personal details. Providing multiple payment options also increases your chances of making a sale since it caters to a variety of preferences.

## Gathering Essential Files for Your Book

Once your book cover is ready, ensure you have various formats for different uses. Your designer should provide you with:

- **Low-resolution JPG:** Ideal for social media and quick online sharing.
- **High-resolution JPG:** Perfect for use on your website and blog.
- **PDF:** Required for print media, including magazines and newspapers.
- **3D Mockups:** Great for promotional material, such as flyers and digital advertisements.

These files ensure your book looks professional across all platforms. Free tools like **Canva.com** and **BookBrush.com** can help you create additional fun promotional images using these covers.

**Start Developing Your Website:** Your author website is your digital home base. It should not only showcase your book but also capture leads and provide valuable content. Adding a **Book** tab is essential for directing readers to purchase options and informing them about potential book club visits.

One key aspect of your website should be a **lead magnet**—a free download or resource that encourages visitors to join your email list. This can be anything from a free chapter of your book, a guide, or exclusive content related to your book's theme. Lead magnets are crucial for building an audience and maintaining engagement.

**Joining Media and Podcast Platforms:** Visibility is key. Joining platforms like **SourceBottle** and **PitchRate** will allow you to connect with reporters seeking experts and authors for their stories. Additionally, placing your profile on podcast platforms like **Matchmaker.fm** and **Podmatch.com** opens doors to guest appearances, where you can promote your book to targeted audiences.

**Engage on Social Media:** Your online presence should include at least one or two active social media profiles. Platforms like **X**, **Facebook, LinkedIn, Instagram,** and **YouTube** offer unique ways to connect with readers and fellow authors. Consistent posting and genuine engagement are essential for growing your audience.

**Join Goodreads:** Create a **Reader** account on Goodreads to start interacting with other readers. This is a fantastic platform for recommending books, joining discussions, and eventually transitioning to an **Author** profile once your book is live.

## Start Developing Your Author Website

Your author website is the cornerstone of your online platform and book marketing efforts. Whether you have an existing business website or are creating a brand-new one, it should act as your primary hub where potential readers, media, and industry contacts can find all relevant information about your book.

## For Existing Websites

If you already have a website for your business, you can simply create a **Book Page** within it. This page should be clean, uncluttered, and easy to navigate, allowing visitors to quickly learn about your book. Here's what to include:

- **Book Cover:** Feature an image of your book cover with a hyperlink to your Amazon sales page for easy purchasing.
- **Videos:** Post a short video of you reading an excerpt from your book to give readers a personal connection to your work.
- **Testimonials & Awards:** If you've received endorsements or won awards, include them here for credibility.
- **Book Club Visits:** Offer to visit book clubs by promoting this on your page, which can help you directly engage with readers.
- **Contact Link:** Ensure there's a straightforward way for visitors to contact you, such as a direct link to your email address.

- **Search Engine Optimization (SEO):** Sprinkle relevant keywords throughout the page to make it easy for search engines to index your content and drive organic traffic.

During your book launch, consider making this **Book Page** the landing page on your website. Alternatively, place a prominent announcement on your home page with a glowing testimonial or review, linking back to the **Book Page**.

### Creating an Author Page (if you don't have an existing site)

If you don't already have a website, building a dedicated **Author Website** is essential. You don't need to spend a fortune; many platforms offer affordable, professional-looking templates that can be customized to suit your branding. Here are a few options:

- GoDaddy
- WIX
- WordPress

These platforms provide easy-to-use tools, and many come with drag-and-drop functionality, making it simple to build a website that matches your style without any coding knowledge.

### Website Tips

If you're not comfortable creating a website on your own, you can hire a web designer through platforms like **Fiverr**, where freelancers offer affordable services, often for as little as $50. Alternatively, you could work with established web design services that specialize in author websites to ensure a polished, professional result.

### Maximizing Your Website's Impact

Once your website is live, ensure you continually update it with new content—whether it's a blog, interviews, or upcoming events. Keep readers engaged and give them reasons to return to your site. Additionally, encourage email sign-ups by offering a **lead magnet** like a free chapter, exclusive content, or a discount on pre-orders.

Your website is an extension of your author brand, so make sure it reflects the same professionalism, tone, and care you put into your book. Whether visitors are discovering your work for the first time or longtime readers are returning for updates, your website should make a lasting impression.

## Basic Website Pages

- **Home Page**: Feature your latest book cover, a professional headshot, and a short bio. Add a clear contact tab.
- **About Page**: Include a longer bio and personal headshot.
- **Media Page**: Add a media kit that includes author bios (150 and 300 words), book synopsis, sample interview questions, review excerpts, and headshots.
- **Blog**: Regular blog posts can help engage readers and boost SEO. Archive past posts to show your expertise.
- **Book Club Page**: If your book is great for book clubs, offer to visit clubs either in person or via Zoom.
- **Speaking Page**: If you're a speaker, add testimonials, a promo video, and a list of events.
- **Email Subscription Box**: Include this on every page, offering a valuable gift (like a free chapter) in exchange for emails.
- **Contact Page**: Provide an easy way for readers, collaborators, or event organizers to reach you. Include a simple form for inquiries, collaborations, or speaking engagements.
- **Newsletter Sign-up**: Include a form for visitors to subscribe to your email list. Offer an incentive like a free short story or exclusive content to encourage sign-ups. This is crucial for building a dedicated readership.

- **E-commerce Functionality:** If selling directly, ensure your website integrates e-commerce solutions like WooCommerce, Squarespace's store, or Wix Stores. This enables you to sell physical and digital books directly to readers.

## Promote and Protect

- **Links to Social Media**: Make it easy for readers to find you on Facebook, X, YouTube, LinkedIn, Pinterest, and Instagram.
- **Copyright Protection**: Protect your content by adding a copyright statement at the bottom of each page (e.g., "Copyright © 2025 Your Name. All Rights Reserved").

## Lead Magnets and Free Gifts

To build your email list, offer free, high-value items such as:

- Podcasts
- Webinars in your expertise
- Checklists
- Reference guides
- Creative infographics

## Maximizing Sales Through Amazon

When selling books, link all sales to Amazon to boost your rankings, but also offer the option for bulk or signed book purchases directly through a contact link on your website. For bulk or signed orders, handle payments via **Square** or **PayPal** and charge for shipping.

## Shipping Tips

When shipping books, use **media mail** for cheaper rates but avoid adding notes or extra materials, as media mail only covers the books themselves.

## Author Website Builders

Here's a breakdown of the top tools and how to build an effective website using each platform.

### WordPress for Author Websites

**What it is:**
WordPress is a highly customizable, open-source website-building platform that gives authors control over every aspect of their site. It's popular due to its flexibility, allowing authors to create websites that are SEO-friendly and tailored to their specific branding needs.

**Why use it:**
WordPress is perfect for authors who want a site that can grow with them. Its vast range of plugins and themes allows for extensive customization, making it ideal for everything from blogging to selling books.

### Steps to Create a WordPress Author Website

1. **Choose a Domain Name:**
   Your domain name is essentially your online address, so it should reflect your author brand. Ideally, you'll want something easy to remember, like yourname.com, to help readers find you easily.

2. **Select Hosting:**
   Hosting is the server where your website's data is stored. Choose a reliable provider like **Bluehost** or **SiteGround** that offers good uptime and customer support. Hosting is a crucial part of ensuring your website runs smoothly.

3. **Install WordPress:**
   Most hosting services provide a one-click installation process for WordPress. Once installed, you'll have access to the platform's content management system (CMS), which allows you to create and organize your website's pages.

4. **Choose a Theme:**
    Themes control the look and feel of your website. Select a theme that is responsive (works well on mobile devices) and tailored for authors. Popular choices include **Astra** and **Author Pro,** which are easy to customize and designed with writers in mind.
5. **Install Plugins:**
    Plugins are add-ons that expand your site's functionality. Install essential plugins like **Yoast SEO** (to improve search engine rankings) and **WooCommerce** (to sell books directly). These plugins will help optimize your site's performance and increase sales potential.

## Squarespace for Author Websites

**What it is:**

Squarespace is a user-friendly website builder that offers beautiful, professional templates, making it a favorite among authors who want a quick setup with built-in features like e-commerce.

**Why use it:**

For authors who don't have technical skills but want an elegant website, Squarespace provides everything from easy drag-and-drop designs to built-in options for selling books online.

## Steps to Create a Squarespace Author Website

1. **Sign Up:**
    Start by choosing a plan—whether personal or business—depending on your needs. A personal plan is enough if you're not focusing heavily on selling merchandise or books. For more advanced marketing tools, the business plan offers additional features.
2. **Select a Template:**
    Squarespace offers a range of visually appealing templates. Select one that resonates with your author brand and genre. For example, if you write contemporary

romance, a template with soft colors and clean fonts could be fitting. Their drag-and-drop builder makes customizing the look easy without needing coding skills.

3. **Customize the Layout:**
Use Squarespace's intuitive drag-and-drop editor to personalize your site. Add elements like images of your book covers, author photos, text about your writing journey, and call-to-action buttons that lead visitors to buy your books.

4. **Create Essential Pages:**
Ensure your website has the following key pages:
    - **About Page:** Share your story as an author, your journey, and your goals.
    - **Books Page:** Display all your books with descriptions, purchase links, and reviews.
    - **Blog:** Engage readers with updates, insights, or behind-the-scenes content.
    - **Contact Page:** Provide an easy way for readers, media, or industry professionals to contact you.

5. **Set Up E-commerce:**
Enable Squarespace's built-in online store feature to sell your books directly from the website. You can accept payments using popular platforms like PayPal or Stripe. E-commerce also allows for digital product sales like eBooks and audiobooks.

6. **Connect a Domain:**
You can either register a new domain name directly through Squarespace or connect an existing one. The domain should reflect your author brand, such as **yourname.com**, to make it easy for readers to find you.

7. **Launch Your Site:**
Before going live, test your website's functionality, checking things like purchase buttons, links, and mobile optimization. Once everything looks and works perfectly, publish your site and promote it to your audience.

## Wix for Author Websites

**What it is:**

Wix is a website builder known for its drag-and-drop editor, making it perfect for authors who are new to web design but want a professional, functional site without needing coding skills.

**Why use it:**

Wix offers flexibility and ease, ideal for authors who want a quick and straightforward setup while still having access to advanced features like e-commerce and SEO tools.

**Steps to Create a Wix Author Website**

1. **Create an Account:**
   Sign up for Wix with either a free or paid plan, depending on your needs. The free plan provides basic functionality, while the paid plans offer more features like custom domain connections and additional storage.

2. **Choose a Template:**
   Wix offers a variety of templates designed specifically for authors and creatives. Select a template that reflects your writing style or genre, ensuring it has a clean, professional look.

3. **Customize with the Editor:**
   Use the intuitive drag-and-drop editor to personalize your website. You can easily add text, images, videos, and even galleries of book covers or writing samples. The editor is beginner-friendly, allowing you to rearrange elements effortlessly.

4. **Add Essential Pages:**
   Ensure your site includes the core pages.

5. **Set Up E-commerce:**
   With Wix Stores, you can sell your books directly from your site. This feature allows you to set up an online store where visitors can purchase both physical and

digital copies of your books. You can also track orders and manage your inventory.

6. **Optimize for SEO:**
   Wix has built-in SEO tools that guide you through improving your site's search engine ranking. Use these tools to ensure your website is discoverable by readers searching for your genre or specific books.

7. **Publish Your Site:**
   Once you've completed your design, tested your site's functionality, and optimized it for SEO, you can publish it. After going live, promote your website through social media platforms, newsletters, and email lists to drive traffic.

## Riley-Infinity Author Websites

For a more customized, all-in-one platform, Riley-Infinity Publishing Services offers tailored author website creation. These sites can be adjusted to your specific needs, whether you're focusing on selling books, building a community, or growing your brand as an author.

## How to Sell Books Directly from Your Website

1. **Set Up E-commerce**
   Choose an e-commerce platform such as WooCommerce (for WordPress), Squarespace's built-in store, or Wix Stores to handle book sales directly from your website.

2. **Payment Processing**
   Integrate secure payment gateways like PayPal, Stripe, or Square to accept payments for your books. These platforms provide simple and trusted payment solutions for customers.

3. **Product Listings**
   Create professional product listings for each of your books. Include cover images, detailed descriptions, and pricing information for both digital and physical copies.

4. **Shipping Options**
   Set up shipping options for physical books. Define rates based on location or offer free shipping as a promotion.

5. **Promotions**
   Run special promotions such as discount codes, bundles (e.g., signed copies with exclusive content), or limited-time offers to drive sales and reward loyal customers.

6. **Direct Links**
   Ensure that "Buy Now" buttons are clearly visible on your website, and use compelling calls to action to guide users to purchase your books directly.

7. **Customer Follow-Up**
   After making a sale, follow up with a thank-you email. Invite customers to join your mailing list for updates on future releases or exclusive offers, enhancing your reader relationship and encouraging repeat business.

For authors seeking a seamless and elevated digital experience, our fully integrated websites go beyond book sales. These custom sites can include built-in features like social media feeds, blog integration, call and text capabilities, and automated customer engagement tools—all designed to help you connect with readers, grow your audience, and manage your author brand from one central hub. You can even choose to have AI on your website selling your book for you and setting appointments for your course you may choose to create on the platform. Whether you're launching your first book or scaling your author platform, an integrated site ensures your online presence is as dynamic and engaging as your writing, and if you need social media management and content creation, well, we have you there too!

# CHAPTER 4

# ENGAGING YOUR AUDIENCE EARLY

**Building Your Email List with a Lead Magnet**

One of the most important assets you can build as an author is your email list. Engaging your audience early allows you to cultivate a direct relationship with your readers, letting them know about new releases, special promotions, and updates. The sooner you start, the better.

**Why Start Early?**

Your book might be your biggest achievement, but your email list is your biggest marketing asset. Having an email list gives you direct access to your audience, allowing you to send targeted messages that can turn into book sales, event registrations, or valuable word-of-mouth promotion.

## Steps to Build Your List

1. **Create an Email Sign-up Form:** Place a visible sign-up form on your website. This should appear on every page to maximize its reach.

2. **Start a Newsletter:** Use tools like **Constant Contact** or **MailChimp** to create a professional newsletter. A great way to keep your audience engaged is to send regular updates, exclusive content, or even behind-the-scenes looks at your writing process. Offering an opt-in form on your website will make it easy for people to subscribe.

3. **Free E-Gifts:** Entice visitors to join your email list by offering a **valuable gift**. Examples include:
   - A podcast episode where you share insights or stories related to your book.
   - A webinar showcasing your expertise on the book's subject matter.
   - A checklist or reference guide full of tips and tools related to your topic.
   - Fun, creative infographics or exclusive resources.

By giving away something valuable, you're showing potential readers that you appreciate their time and interest, while simultaneously building your subscriber base. If you are looking for an integrated platform with everything, we can help you there as well.

## Speaking Engagements

When you have speaking events, always offer an email sign-up sheet at the back of the room or table. Many attendees will gladly give you their email addresses if you follow up with valuable information or special offers related to your presentation or book.

## Tools and Services to Help You Build Your List

Many website design companies and email services like **MailChimp** and **Constant Contact** offer tools to help you build, manage, and engage with your email list. These platforms provide easy-to-use features, including custom email templates that match your branding. Some programs, like **Constant Contact's Essentials Program,** even offer templates that mirror your website design, creating a seamless experience for your subscribers.

## Maximizing Engagement

Once you've gathered emails, nurture your relationship with your audience by sending out consistent, engaging content. Whether it's sneak peeks of your book, writing tips, or updates on your author journey, regular interaction keeps your audience engaged and more likely to support your future projects.

**Create a "Book Club" Tab on Your Website** Adding a dedicated **Book Club** tab to your website is a great way to encourage reader interaction. Many readers enjoy discussing books in groups, and by promoting your availability for virtual book club visits (via Zoom or other platforms), you increase your reach. This tab should include information about your book, how to book you for a virtual visit, and any additional resources to enhance the reading experience, such as discussion guides or video messages.

**Boost Visibility with SourceBottle and PitchRate** to increase media visibility. These platforms connect you with journalists, bloggers, and media outlets looking for experts in various fields. By positioning yourself as an expert in your book's subject matter, you can gain media coverage and valuable exposure, driving readers to your book and boosting credibility.

**Open and Engage on Social Media** Social media is an invaluable tool for engaging with your audience early. Set up accounts on platforms where your readers are most active, such as **X, Facebook, Instagram, LinkedIn,** and **YouTube.** Consistency is key—regularly post updates about your book, share behind-the-scenes content, and encourage interaction through questions or polls.

Each platform serves a unique purpose:

- **Facebook**: Ideal for engaging in deeper conversations with your followers. Create polls, host Q&A sessions, or join book-related groups.
- **X**: A great platform for short, impactful updates. Use X to engage in trending topics or share snippets from your book.
- **Instagram**: A visual platform where you can share cover reveals, behind-the-scenes content, and even short video clips.
- **LinkedIn**: Particularly useful for nonfiction authors, LinkedIn allows you to establish yourself as an expert and build a professional network.
- **YouTube**: If you're comfortable in front of the camera, consider vlogging about your writing journey or sharing book trailers.

**Start a Blog on Medium.com** To further establish yourself as an expert, consider starting a blog on **Medium.com**. Medium offers an open platform for writers, experts, and thought leaders to share articles and ideas. By publishing content related to your book's topic, you can develop a following, build credibility, and use your blog as an extension of your marketing strategy.

Here are a few ways blogging benefits you:

1. **Reputation Building**: You position yourself as a thought leader, giving readers a reason to come back for more insights.
2. **Community Engagement**: Interact with your followers through comments and responses to build a stronger connection.
3. **Content for Future Books**: Regular blogging keeps you on top of your field, generating ideas and material for your next book.
4. **Global Reach**: Blogging spreads your content across the web, increasing visibility.

5. **Search Engine Optimization (SEO)**: Consistently publishing quality content helps improve your website's search engine ranking, making it easier for readers to find you.

## Repurpose Content Across Platforms

Once you publish a blog, you can repurpose the content across your social media platforms. For example, a detailed blog post can be condensed into a tweet for X, a visual summary for Instagram, or a conversation starter on Facebook. Repurposing content maximizes its value and reaches different audience segments without extra effort.

## Open Social Media Accounts and Start Engaging

Social media is one of the most effective tools for connecting with your audience and building a tribe around your book. Start by identifying the platforms where your target audience is most active. Here's how you can approach some key platforms:

## Facebook

Instead of starting an author page, which gets low organic traffic due to Facebook's algorithm, consider adding book content to your personal or business page. Optimize your presence by:

1. Joining **Facebook Groups** related to your book's topic.
2. Engaging in conversations to build your reputation as an expert.
3. Starting your own group to connect with your audience.

Facebook Groups offer the opportunity to interact with your target readers by answering questions, participating in discussions, and becoming a trusted voice in your field. If your book is about parenting, for example, join parenting groups and offer advice based on your book's subject matter without directly pitching it.

## X

X allows you to connect with both influencers and a broader audience. Start by creating a consistent profile with branding that aligns with your other platforms. Use a 142-character synopsis of who you are and what you offer, and include a link to your website or Amazon page.

**Three Primary X Strategies:**

1. **Marketing to the Masses:** Share valuable content, book-related news, and insights that position you as a go-to source for information.
2. **Trend Spotting:** Keep an eye on trending topics that relate to your book, and engage in these discussions to increase your visibility.
3. **Connecting with Influencers:** Reach out to industry influencers and thought leaders via direct tweets to build connections.

Using relevant hashtags, such as #amwriting, can help you find and connect with other authors and readers. By joining trending conversations, you have the opportunity to reach a large audience with a single well-timed tweet.

## LinkedIn

LinkedIn is especially valuable for nonfiction authors or professionals who want to establish authority in their field. To make the most of LinkedIn:

1. **Optimize Your Profile:** Use keywords and add photos, awards, and videos that reflect your work.
2. **Post Your Book:** Include a link to your Amazon sales page.
3. **Join LinkedIn Groups:** Engage in discussions and provide value in areas related to your book's topic.
4. **Ask for Testimonials:** Request past clients or colleagues to leave endorsements, which help build credibility.

## Instagram

Instagram is a visual platform where authors can share behind-the-scenes content, book snippets, and personal stories. Use a combination of posts, stories, and live sessions to engage with your audience. Ensure your posts are easy to read and shareable by using clear visuals and compelling captions.

**Tips for Instagram:**

- Use relevant hashtags to increase reach.
- Collaborate with other authors by sharing each other's content or hosting live discussions.
- Post personal content that helps followers connect with you on a deeper level.

## Blogging on Medium.com

For authors, **Medium.com** is a great platform for sharing long-form content, articles, or stories related to your book's topic. Publishing regularly on Medium helps build your reputation, engages your audience, and enhances your book's visibility. Each post should tie back to your book, linking to your Amazon sales page.

**Key Benefits of Blogging:**

- Establish yourself as an expert in your niche.
- Interact with readers and build a community.
- Stockpile content for future books by staying current in your field.

## Engagement Tools and Resources

To make the most of your social media efforts, utilize design tools to create professional images and posts. Free services like **Canva** and **PicMonkey** allow even beginners to design visually appealing content for social media.

**FREE Author Items List:**

- **Canva.com:** Create engaging visuals.
- **Fiverr.com:** Find freelancers to help with logos, headers, and more.
- **Buffer.com/Pablo:** A scheduling tool for social media management.

## YouTube

YouTube offers a visual platform that can help you connect with readers through dynamic content. Start by creating a custom-designed **YouTube channel** with a branded background, profile, and keywords relevant to your book. You don't need to be a video expert to make YouTube work for you—simple, authentic videos can have a great impact.

- **What to Post:**
  - Clips from speaking engagements
  - Excerpts of you reading from your book
  - Reader testimonials about your book

Keep videos short and engaging, ranging from **thirty seconds to three minutes**. Don't forget to add relevant keywords in the descriptions to increase discoverability. You can hire a designer on **Fiverr** if you want professional help with your channel design.

## Goodreads

Goodreads is the ultimate social platform for book lovers, and it provides great tools to help you reach your target audience. Set up a **Goodreads Reader account** before your book launches. This will allow you to engage with readers, build your presence, and interact with potential fans before you officially launch as an author.

## ENGAGING YOUR AUDIENCE EARLY

Six Ways to Engage on Goodreads:

1. **Import your friends from Facebook or X** – This helps you build connections quickly.
2. **Leave reviews for books you love** – Your activity will attract other readers.
3. **Comment on posts from other readers** – Engage in conversations about books and genres.
4. **Share your favorite books** – Show your audience what inspires you.
5. **Invite readers in your genre to be friends** – Build connections with people who share your interests.
6. **Join groups in your genre** – Participate in discussions relevant to your book's themes.

Goodreads also allows authors to interact with their audience in a more book-centric way. Take full advantage of their **Author account** once your book is launched, optimizing your profile and engaging with your growing fan base.

### Blogging on Medium.com

If you're looking for a platform where long-form content shines, **medium.com** is ideal. With millions of monthly readers, Medium is an excellent space for sharing articles, stories, and insights related to your book's subject. Nonfiction authors, in particular, can build a strong reputation by regularly publishing thoughtful, relevant articles that tie back to their book. Always include a byline with a link to your book on Amazon, which helps you generate traffic and sales.

### Engagement Beyond Social Media

To increase visibility, sign up for platforms like **SourceBottle, Qwoted,** and **PitchRate,** which connect you with journalists and bloggers looking for expert commentary. Becoming a guest on podcasts through sites like **PodMatch** or **Matchmaker.fm** can also boost your credibility and introduce your book to new audiences.

**Qwoted, PitchRate,** and **SourceBottle** are platforms designed to connect you with journalists, bloggers, and media professionals looking for expert quotes or stories. As an author, these platforms offer you the chance to showcase your expertise and gain media coverage.

**How to Use Qwoted:**

1. Sign up for free at **qwoted.com.**
2. Select your expertise categories to filter relevant media opportunities.
3. Receive real-time query notifications or browse live opportunities, then respond with a tailored pitch showcasing your expertise.

**How to Use PitchRate:**

1. Register at **pitchrate.com.**
2. Create a pitch showcasing your book and its unique value.
3. Submit your pitch to media outlets for coverage opportunities.

**How to Use SourceBottle:**

1. Sign up for free at **sourcebottle.com.**
2. Select categories relevant to your book's topic (e.g., publishing, lifestyle, or health).
3. Receive email alerts with media queries and respond to those that align with your book's theme or expertise.

Qwoted and PitchRate allow you to build credibility and gain exposure by being featured in media outlets or podcasts, which can be especially useful in the weeks leading up to your launch. SourceBottle connects you to those same items, plus bloggers and content creators.

### Engage a PR Professional

PR can make a significant difference in getting your book the attention it deserves. There are companies that specialize in helping self-published authors with media coverage, interviews, and more. Consider hiring PR professionals like those listed below:

- **SpeakerTunity:** Offers media kit training, podcast leads, and speaking engagement lists. They also provide training on how to create and utilize a media kit.
- **Smith Publicity:** Marissa at Smith Publicity understands self-published authors and can position your book for success, starting a few months before your launch.
- **Triangle Media:** Suzanne Lynn specializes in crafting media packages and conducting professional interviews you can use for marketing your book.

### Create a Book Trailer Video

A well-crafted book trailer video can captivate your audience and serve as a powerful marketing tool. Keep it short—under ninety seconds—while highlighting your book's plot, themes, or emotional appeal. Platforms like **Animoto** or **Canva** offer user-friendly tools to create professional-looking videos.

### Submit for Trade Reviews and Endorsements

Trade reviews and endorsements are essential for building credibility, especially before your book is released. Consider submitting your manuscript to:

- **Kirkus Reviews**
- **Booklist**
- **Foreword Reviews**

Additionally, reach out to industry experts or influencers in your genre to provide a quote or endorsement that can be included on your book cover or website.

## Start Your Social Media Twenty-One-Day Countdown to Book Launch

Social media is crucial for building hype. Plan a twenty-one-day countdown before your launch using the following strategies:

1. **Days 21–15:** Teasers (e.g., cover reveals, snippets, character bios).
2. **Days 14–7:** Behind-the-scenes content (e.g., your writing process, research).
3. **Day 6–Launch Day:** Announcements of pre-orders, giveaways, and book launch events.

Use platforms like **Hootsuite** or **Buffer** to schedule posts across multiple social media channels.

## Prepare a Book One-Sheet, Bookmarks, and Postcards

Having physical promotional materials for in-person events or sending to reviewers is vital. Create:

- **Book One-Sheet:** A one-page document summarizing your book, including the synopsis, genre, author bio, and release date.
- **Bookmarks and Postcards:** These should feature your book cover, a tagline, and purchase links.

Tools like **Vistaprint** can help create these materials affordably.

## Write and Distribute a Press Release

A press release is a concise, professional announcement about your upcoming book. It should include:

- **Headline:** Capture attention with a strong headline.
- **Summary:** Briefly describe your book and why it's noteworthy.
- **Body:** Provide details about the release, endorsements, and where readers can purchase the book.

Submit your press release to local media outlets, relevant bloggers, and online press release distribution services such as **PRWeb** or **PressRelease.com**.

## Plan Your Book Launch Party

Whether in person or virtual, a book launch party is a fantastic way to celebrate your book's release while engaging with readers. Key planning tips include:

1. **Venue:** Choose a bookstore, local café, or online via Zoom or Facebook Live.
2. **Invite Guests:** Send invitations to friends, family, influencers, and media.
3. **Activities:** Include a short reading, Q&A, giveaways, and time for book signings (or personalized messages in virtual events).

# CHAPTER 5

## PREPARING FOR LAUNCH

As you approach the final stages of book production, preparation for launch becomes crucial to ensure a successful release. This chapter will guide you through essential prelaunch activities, including creating promotional content, engaging with early readers, and setting the stage for your book's big debut.

### Cataloging in Publication (CIP)

Cataloging in Publication (CIP) data can be an essential tool for marketing your book to libraries and bookstores, even though it's not strictly necessary for book sales. This bibliographic record provides crucial information about your book to librarians, making it easier for them to catalog and recommend it.

The **Library of Congress** offers CIP data, but due to high demand, self-published books are often excluded. If your book doesn't qualify for CIP, you can opt for **P-CIP** (Publisher's Cataloging in Publication), which serves a similar purpose. This data is particularly helpful if you're aiming for library distribution. You can obtain a P-CIP from various professional services for a fee, which makes your book more accessible to librarians.

## Use Your Book's Back Cover Content

The back cover of your book is valuable marketing real estate and should be used strategically. Beyond the acknowledgments and glossary, the back matter can promote your other books, services, or workshops and even encourage readers to connect with you. Here are some effective ways to use this space:

- **Promote yourself as a speaker**: Include details about workshops or speaking engagements that tie into your book's theme.
- **Offer book club visits**: If your book fits well with book clubs, invite readers to have you attend their meetings virtually or in person.
- **Highlight your other works**: Use the back cover to direct readers to your other books or upcoming releases.
- **Promote a charity**: If your book supports a cause, include information about a related charity.
- **Use QR codes**: Add QR codes that link to a free resource or a special video message from you. This is a great way to engage readers and collect email addresses for future marketing.

Incorporating these elements in the back matter helps keep your readers engaged even after they finish the book and provides avenues for further connection and promotion. It also ensures you're maximizing every inch of your book's content for marketing and engagement purposes.

## Create a Book Trailer

A **book trailer** is a short, engaging video designed to entice potential readers by offering a cinematic glimpse into your book. Think of it as a movie trailer for your story, drawing viewers in with compelling visuals and sound. It's an excellent marketing tool that can be shared across social media platforms, your Amazon Author Central page, and your website.

**Tips for Creating a Book Trailer:**

1. **DIY with iMovie:** If you're tech-savvy, use **iMovie** to create your own book trailer. Keep it fun and intriguing—avoid making it feel like a hard sell.
2. **Hire a Freelancer on Fiverr:** Platforms like **Fiverr.com** offer book trailer services. Be sure to hire experienced creators with positive reviews for the best results.
3. **PowerPoint to Video:** Use PowerPoint to create a slide show and convert it to a video. Add background music to enhance the atmosphere.
4. **Use Lumen5:** A free tool like **Lumen5** can help create quick, professional-looking trailers.
5. **Canva: Canva.com** now offers tools to make book trailers, providing customizable templates and simple editing tools.

**TIP:** Avoid including text like "Coming Soon!" unless you have the ability to update the trailer once your book is published.

## ARC Reviews (Advance Reader Copies)

One of the most powerful tools in your prelaunch arsenal is **ARC reviews.** These advance reader copies allow you to generate buzz, collect professional reviews, and secure endorsements before your official release. Reviews lend credibility and can drive sales once the book is published.

**Steps to Get ARC Reviews:**

1. Ensure your book is fully **edited, formatted,** and has its **cover design** complete.
2. Add the phrase **"Advance Reader Copy"** (ARC) to your book cover.
3. For the back cover, leave space for future **reviews** once they come in.
4. Print **five to twenty ARC copies** and send them to professional reviewers, influencers, or well-known endorsers.
5. Once you receive the reviews, embed the **best ones** on the back or front cover.
6. After your ARCs are finalized, you'll be ready for the official **launch**.

Taking the extra time to send out ARCs three to four months before your launch gives your book an edge, providing visibility and validation in the market before the big day.

**FREE Author Items List**

Consider using free tools like **Canva** or **Lumen5** to create your book trailers, while platforms like **NetGalley** or **BookSirens** are excellent for distributing ARCs to readers and influencers who can help spread the word before your launch. These tools allow you to create polished promotional materials without breaking the bank, while generating buzz for your upcoming release.

**Collecting Testimonials for Your Book**

When preparing your book for launch, collecting **testimonials** from recognized individuals in your genre or industry can significantly boost your book's credibility. Testimonials, also known as endorsements, serve as social proof, showing potential readers that respected figures endorse your work. These testimonials can be placed on the **front cover, back cover, Amazon page,** or the **"Praise** for" section** in the front matter of your book, as well as in your overall marketing materials.

## Why Testimonials Matter

Testimonials are crucial for gaining the trust of readers who may not be familiar with you or your work. A strong endorsement from a notable figure adds an element of authority and validation to your book, helping it stand out in a crowded marketplace. When readers see a testimonial from someone they recognize or respect, they are more likely to take your book seriously and, ultimately, make a purchase.

While reaching out to celebrities or industry leaders may seem intimidating, you might be surprised how willing some are to support emerging authors. Many high-profile individuals enjoy lending a hand to rising talents, especially if your book aligns with their own interests or causes.

## When to Request Testimonials

Ideally, you should start reaching out for testimonials once your manuscript has been fully edited and proofread. Some authors wait until the book's layout is complete, as this gives potential endorsers a more polished version to review. Regardless of the timing, it's important to give your potential endorsers enough time to respond before your launch.

## How to Reach Out

Reaching out for testimonials requires tact and professionalism. Social media, particularly platforms like X, can be effective for contacting celebrities or influencers. X, for example, has fewer restrictions on direct communication, making it easier to engage with individuals who might otherwise be hard to reach. However, your message needs to be concise and respectful. Avoid lengthy explanations or gushing compliments—keep it professional, sincere, and to the point.

Here's a simple approach:

- **Start with a compliment:** Mention a specific detail about their work that has inspired you.
- **Be brief:** No one has time to read a long email. Get to the point quickly.
- **Offer pre-written testimonials:** Make the process easier for them by offering several one-sentence testimonials to choose from. It's likely that their assistant or manager will glance through your request, so providing pre-written options increases your chances of receiving a testimonial.

Sample Request Template

Here is an example of how you can request a testimonial or endorsement:

Dear [Name],

I've been an admirer of your work, especially [mention a specific project or quality about their work that inspires you]. Your journey and achievements have been a great source of inspiration for me as I work on my book, [Book Title], which is set to be released in [release date].

I would be honored if you would consider providing a short testimonial for my book. I've attached a press-ready file and a brief synopsis for your reference.

To make things easier, I've included a few sample testimonials below. Feel free to use one as it is, combine elements, or write your own if you feel inspired:

1. Testimonial option 1
2. Testimonial option 2
3. Testimonial option 3

Please let me know by [deadline], and include how you would like your name and title to appear.

Thank you so much for your time and consideration.

Warm regards,
[Your Name]
[Your Contact Information]

# CHAPTER 6

## GAINING CREDIBILITY AND REVIEWS

When launching your book, building credibility through reviews is crucial for gaining traction in a competitive market. Reviews, both free and paid, help you establish trust with potential readers and gain visibility with important industry players like libraries, bookstores, and reviewers. Here are some essential strategies to help you secure valuable reviews before and after your book launch.

**NetGalley Marketing Program**

The **NetGalley Marketing Program** is an outstanding platform for authors to share advance copies (galleys) of their books with a network of over 215,000 influential reviewers, including bloggers, librarians, booksellers, and media professionals. NetGalley provides a secure, anti-copying format for sharing your galleys digitally, ensuring your work is protected while receiving critical feedback and reviews.

Though it requires a six-month membership and a marketing budget (costs range from $349 to $599 at the time of writing), many authors agree that it's worth the investment. The visibility and feedback gained from the NetGalley platform can significantly improve your book's marketability.

**NetGalley Co-ops:** For authors on a budget, **NetGalley co-ops** offer an affordable alternative. These co-ops allow a group of authors to share the cost of using NetGalley, making it more manageable. Many companies also offer to manage the co-op process so you can focus on your book launch. A quick online search for "NetGalley co-ops" will provide several options for affordable group plans.

Trade Reviews

Securing reviews from industry trade publications such as **Publishers Weekly, Kirkus,** or **Library Journal** can be a game-changer for your book. These trades prefer to review books four to six months before publication, so early planning is essential. Although submissions are free, the competition is steep, and many books do not make the cut for free trade reviews due to the high volume of submissions.

**How to Submit to Trade Reviews:**

- Booklist (booklistonline.com)
- Kirkus Reviews (kirkusreviews.com)
- Library Journal (reviews.libraryjournal.com)
- Foreword Reviews (forewordreviews.com)
- Publishers Weekly (publishersweekly.com)

These publications offer massive credibility and exposure, especially if you're able to secure a spot. However, because the odds of being selected are slim, you may want to explore **paid trade reviews** to guarantee visibility.

## GAINING CREDIBILITY AND REVIEWS

Paid Trade Reviews

While there is some debate over whether authors should pay for reviews, many experts and seasoned authors believe that paid reviews from reputable sources are well worth the investment. It's important to remember that paying for a review doesn't mean buying a good review—it means paying for an **honest** and professional assessment. Paid reviews not only appear in their respective publications but are also distributed to bookstores, libraries, agents, and even big publishers.

Here are three respected services for **paid trade reviews**:

- **Kirkus Indie Reviews** (kirkusreviews.com/author-services/indie): Known for its honest, in-depth reviews, Kirkus is one of the most trusted names in the industry.
- **Book Life** (booklife.com): Offers professional reviews and features your book in a highly respected database.
- **Blue Ink Review** (blueinkreview.com): Specializes in indie books, providing professional reviews and enhanced credibility.

Additionally, some reviewers offer **combo specials**, which include expedited reviews and additional services, making this a great option for authors looking to boost their visibility quickly.

1. Create Book Postcards or Bookmarks
   Book postcards or bookmarks are an essential part of your marketing toolkit. They can be used for book signings, giveaways, or as a thank-you for readers.

   - **Design to Match Your Branding:** Your postcard or bookmark should reflect the tone and style of your book. Whether it's sleek and professional or whimsical and fun, ensure it matches your brand.
   - **Include Key Information:** Make sure your contact details, website, and social media handles are

visible. You can also add a favorite quote from the book or a short message to entice readers.

- **Add Imagery:** Include a photo of your book or a headshot of you holding the book to personalize it.

- **Hire a Designer:** If possible, have your book cover designer create these marketing tools for consistency in style. This ensures the design is professional and aligned with the book's aesthetic.

2. Create Business Cards

    If you have a business related to your book's topic, or if you're an author growing your personal brand, business cards are another great tool for networking.

    - **Use a Related Business Card:** If your book ties into a larger business (e.g., coaching, consulting, or another service), simply add "Author of [Your Book's Title]" to your business card.

    - **Make Book-Specific Cards:** If your book stands alone, create a card that focuses solely on your book. Feature the book cover on the back and include information about where to purchase it, along with your contact details.

    - **Showcase a Professional Look:** High-quality paper and a well-designed card give a polished impression to new connections.

3. Make a Poster Board of Your Book Cover

    A large **24" x 36" poster** of your book cover can be a striking visual at any event.

    - **Use for Photo Ops:** Whether at a book launch party, a book signing, or even a book club meeting, this poster serves as a great backdrop for photos and a way to draw attention.

- **Affordable Options:** You can get these printed for as low as $20 at stores like Staples, especially when they have sales or through services like Groupon.

## Tips on How to Write a Press Release

A well-crafted press release can spread the word about your book and increase visibility, but it needs to be handled carefully.

1. **Frame Your Press Release as Newsworthy**
   Press releases work best when positioned as an **event** or **news** rather than just a promotion. Think of a compelling angle: Why should people care about your book?

2. **Keep it Concise**
   A great press release should be between **three hundred and eight hundred words,** with the sweet spot around **four hundred to five hundred words.** Keep it clear, straightforward, and to the point.

3. **Limit the Links**
   Too many links can overwhelm the reader. Stick to **one or two** links at most, preferably to your author website or book landing page.

4. **Use Keywords for SEO**
   Press releases stay online for long periods and are indexed by search engines, making them powerful for **SEO**. Be sure to use relevant keywords in the headline, body, and any quotes.

5. **Get It Proofread**
   Have a **professional proofreader** review your press release. A polished, error-free document looks far more credible.

6. **Follow the Standard Format**
   Press releases are expected to follow a certain structure:
   - Use a **12-point** font in either **Times New Roman** or **Arial**.
   - Keep everything on one side of **8 ½ x 11** paper.

- Use title case for the headline (capitalize the first letter of each major word).
- At the top-left, add **FOR IMMEDIATE RELEASE** in uppercase.

## Components of a Press Release

1. Headline

    Your headline should be concise, informative, and grab attention. Like a newspaper headline, it succinctly conveys the newsworthy aspect of your release.

2. City, State, Month, Day, Year

    This is the standard journalistic format that gives context. It informs the reader of the geographic and temporal relevance of the news.

3. Brief Summary Paragraph

    Think of this as a teaser. It should provide a quick overview of what the press release is about. This is where you summarize why your book launch is newsworthy.

4. Body

    This section is the core of the press release. Announce that your book has been released and detail its significance. Highlight why your book stands out and who the target audience is. Here, it's important to take a journalistic tone—inform rather than promote. For instance, focus on the unique aspects of your story or how it addresses timely issues.

5. Quote

    Adding a quote adds personality and authority to the release. You can include a quote from yourself as the author or from a notable figure or expert in your field. The quote should be insightful and offer perspective on the book's value.

6. Company/Organization/Author Info
   This section is a brief biography that provides background information about you as the author. If you have a company for your self-publishing efforts, this is where you describe it. Readers and media outlets will use this to understand your credentials and background.

7. Contact Info
   Be sure to provide clear contact information. This can be your PR person's details or your own, including name, email, phone number, and mailing address.

8. Conclusion
   At the end of the press release, signal its conclusion with three pound signs (###). This is a standard format indicator that the release has ended.

**Example Press Release Structure**

Here's a sample layout to follow:

FOR IMMEDIATE RELEASE
City, State, Month, Day, Year

[Book Title] Launches, Bringing Fresh Perspective to [Genre/Topic]
[Brief Summary of the book, outlining its theme, unique features, and who would benefit from reading it.]

[City, State] – [Author's Name] is excited to announce the release of [Book Title], a [description: genre/subject] that explores [key topic or storyline]. [The body of the release explains the newsworthiness of the book, why it's timely or important, and the intended audience.]

**Quote from Author or Expert**

"I wrote [Book Title] because [quote that provides insight into your motivation or the book's impact]," says [Author's Name].

## About the Author

[Brief bio about you as an author, including any previous works, awards, or relevant achievements.]

## Contact Information

[Your Name or PR person's name]
[Email address]
[Phone number]
[Website]

9. **Distribute Your Press Release**
   Once you've crafted your press release, you need to get it in front of the right people. Email it to bloggers, reviewers, and media outlets that are relevant to your book's market. Be sure to tailor your message to fit the needs of each outlet you reach out to.

## Press Release Distribution Services

To maximize your reach, consider using press release distribution services. Here are some helpful platforms:

- Send2Press (www.Send2Press.com)
- PRLog (www.PRLog.org)
- PRWeb (www.PRWeb.com)
- 1888PressRelease (www.1888pressrelease.com)
- PR.com (www.PR.com)
- Newswire (www.Newswire.com)
- PR Leads (www.PRLeads.com)
- PR Newswire (www.PRNewswire.com)
- PR Focus (www.PRFocus.com)

**Effective Press Releases Have the Following**

1. **Make It Newsworthy:** Focus on why your book is an event worth covering, not just a promotion.
2. **Be Concise:** Aim for four hundred to five hundred words to keep it digestible for busy journalists and bloggers.
3. **Limit Links:** Include only one or two links in the release, such as to your author website or book page.
4. **Use Keywords:** Ensure your press release is optimized for search engines by including relevant keywords.
5. **Proofread:** Make sure to have a professional proofreader review your press release to avoid errors.
6. **Follow the Standard Format:** Use the traditional structure to make it easy for outlets to feature your release.

# CHAPTER 7

## THE THREE-WEEK SOCIAL MEDIA ROLLOUT PLAN

In the digital age, it's essential to leverage multiple platforms for your book launch. This **three-week social media plan** helps build excitement across **Instagram, LinkedIn, X, Facebook**, and more, keeping your audience engaged while promoting your book.

Day 1: Announce Your Book

Start your rollout with a **big announcement** about your upcoming book. Share a teaser, a brief synopsis, or a cover reveal across all platforms, emphasizing the key message or hook. Use visuals that align with your book's genre.

**Tip:** Post a short teaser video on Instagram, a detailed post on LinkedIn, and a high-energy announcement tweet on X.

## Day 2: Announce Your Hashtag

Create and announce a **book-specific hashtag**. Encourage your audience to use it throughout your campaign to generate buzz. This also helps track engagement and connect readers.

## Day 3: Share a Behind-the-Scenes Photo

Give your audience a look into your writing process by sharing a behind-the-scenes photo or a picture of your workspace. Make it personal by explaining your journey as an author.

## Day 4: Host a Countdown Announcement

Start a **countdown** to your book launch. Share a branded post saying, "17 days until launch!" with your cover, title, and release date.

## Day 5: Post a Quote

Share an impactful **quote** from your book. If it's fiction, choose a line that piques curiosity. For nonfiction, share a memorable tip or insight.

**Tip:** Use Instagram Stories to post a visually appealing quote, and invite followers to share it.

## Day 6: Introduce the Release Party

Start promoting your **book launch party** (online or in person). Share the details and encourage RSVPs.

## Day 7: Share an Excerpt

Post a short, engaging **excerpt** from your book that draws readers in. This could be a cliffhanger or a pivotal moment that sparks interest.

## THE THREE-WEEK SOCIAL MEDIA ROLLOUT PLAN

### Day 8: Take a Poll or Ask a Question

Ask your audience a **book-related question** or create a poll to engage them. For example, ask for their opinion on book cover designs or plot predictions.

### Day 9: Post a Video of Your Reaction to Your Book

Share your reaction to seeing your book for the first time—whether it's a printed copy or a formatted eBook. This is a great way to show emotion and connect with your readers.

### Day 10: Share a Pet Pic

Lighten the mood by posting a picture of your pet with your book or manuscript. This is a great way to add a playful, relatable touch to your rollout.

### Day 11: Share a Testimonial

Post a **testimonial or review** from a trade or beta reader. These reviews add credibility and spark curiosity about the book.

### Day 12: Post a Meme or Creative Post

Use a design tool like **Canva** to create a **meme or graphic** that highlights your book or a message related to its theme.

### Day 13: Introduce a Contest

Launch a **giveaway contest**. Offer prizes like a signed copy or exclusive content for those who engage with your posts or share your book-related hashtag.

### Day 14: Post a Q&A Video

Record a short **Q&A** video answering reader-submitted questions about your book or writing process. Use Instagram Stories or X for quick interaction.

### Day 15: Share a Reader Interview

Post a brief **video interview** with one of your beta readers, sharing their thoughts and excitement about your book.

### Day 16: Unveil the Book Trailer

Share your **book trailer** across all platforms. Make sure it's eye-catching, brief (thirty to forty-five seconds), and teases the plot without giving too much away.

### Day 17: Share a Quote or Excerpt

Reignite interest with another **quote or excerpt**, this time sharing something more emotional or revealing. Make it interactive by asking for readers' reactions.

### Day 18: Launch a Hashtag Challenge

Challenge your audience to participate in a **hashtag challenge** that aligns with your book's theme. For instance, if your book is about travel, ask them to share their favorite travel memories.

### Day 19: Share Reviews from Influencers

If you've connected with influencers, share their **reviews** or comments. Their endorsement helps build credibility and reach a wider audience.

### Day 20: Send a Final Reminder

With one day to go, send a **final reminder** for your book launch party or release date. Share a selfie or behind-the-scenes look to add a personal touch.

### Day 21: Launch Day!

It's launch day! Celebrate by sharing a **party video** or a live post to kick off your release. Encourage everyone to share their copies of your book using your official hashtag. Offer giveaways or rewards to those who engage.

# CHAPTER 8

## LAUNCHING YOUR BOOK

A successful book launch doesn't have to fit a one-size-fits-all approach. Each author has unique goals, resources, and comfort levels when it comes to sharing their work with the world. Here, we break down four customizable celebration options. Feel free to select elements from each to craft the book launch strategy that best fits you.

1. BURST Onto the Scene: Live Launch Party

A live launch party can bring your book into the public eye with flair, creating a memorable event for readers, media, and friends. Hosting at a lively spot such as a local bar, restaurant, or community space can set a festive tone and encourage interaction.

What a BURST launch looks like:

- **Send Invitations and Press Releases**: Notify local media and send press releases to nearby newspapers and magazines to build anticipation.
- **Set the Atmosphere**: Decorate with book-themed elements, hire live music, and plan for a photographer to capture moments.
- **Organize Book Sales**: Have books available for purchase and appoint someone to manage sales while you focus on mingling and signing copies.
- **Appoint an Emcee**: Select a trusted friend to facilitate the event, manage Q&A, and host the event.
- **Create a Short Program**: Give a brief reading, followed by a speech about your book's inspiration or journey, and finish with an audience Q&A.
- **Arrange Interviews**: Use the opportunity to connect with local journalists and media to increase publicity.

This style of launch is ideal for authors who enjoy social events and want to interact directly with their readers.

2. Get Your Online Party On: Virtual Book Launch

A virtual launch party is an accessible, budget-friendly alternative that allows you to reach a global audience. From the comfort of your home, you can invite readers, friends, and family worldwide to join and celebrate.

What an Online Party looks like:

- **Choose a Platform and Send Invitations**: Use platforms like Zoom, Google Meet, or other video conferencing software, and send digital invites through email or social media.

- **Appoint an Emcee:** Select a trusted friend to facilitate the event, manage Q&A, monitor the chat, and share book links to streamline the virtual experience.
- **Plan Interactive Elements:** Include a live reading, discussions, and even games to keep attendees engaged.
- **Make Book Purchasing Easy:** Share direct links in the chat for attendees to purchase the book on Amazon or your author website.
- **Record the Event:** Many online platforms allow you to record the event, creating a memorable video to share on your social channels later.

The online option is perfect for reaching a wider audience without geographic limitations and can be more cost-effective than a physical gathering.

3. Social Media Blitz: Digital Marketing Approach

For authors who prefer a low-key approach, a social media blitz can be a powerful way to launch your book. This strategy involves building anticipation over a series of days or weeks by sharing teasers, insights, and excerpts across social media channels.

**What a Social Media Blitz looks like:**

- **Create a Countdown:** Announce a book release countdown, sharing daily posts with sneak peeks, character profiles, or plot teasers on Instagram, Facebook, LinkedIn, or TikTok.
- **Host Live Events:** Incorporate Instagram or Facebook Lives for brief Q&A sessions or live readings to engage your followers.
- **Collaborate with Influencers:** Partner with bloggers, fellow authors, and influencers to expand your reach through guest posts or social media takeovers.

- **Use Paid Ads Strategically**: Amplify your visibility through targeted Facebook or Instagram ads to reach specific demographics relevant to your genre.
- **Encourage Reviews and Reader Participation**: Invite readers to post reviews or share their own photos of your book with your official hashtag to create community engagement.

A social media blitz can create buzz, increase follower engagement, and attract new readers without the need for in-person events, making it ideal for introverted authors.

### 4. Combo Pack: Hybrid Launch Strategy

A hybrid approach combines elements from various launch options to spread out your release efforts and keep your book top of mind. For instance, you might start with a live launch party, then follow up with a virtual event or extended social media campaign.

**What the Combo Pack looks like:**

- **Stage the Launch**: Begin with a live party to kick off the celebration with a close-knit group of local supporters, followed by a virtual event for out-of-town readers.
- **Follow with a Social Media Push**: After the initial events, maintain momentum through a series of social media posts, sharing highlights, interviews, and special offers.
- **Add Giveaways and Limited-Time Promotions**: Offer giveaways or exclusive discounts during specific phases to keep readers engaged and attract new fans.
- **Host a Post-Launch Q&A**: Use the online format to host a post-launch Q&A a few weeks after your release, allowing time for readers to complete your book and come with questions.

This multi-faceted approach lets you engage with readers in various ways, accommodating those who may not have been able to attend the original event.

## Choosing Your Launch Style

Your launch should reflect your personality, goals, and budget. Each style allows you to connect with your audience and share your work in a way that feels authentic to you. Embrace the strategy that resonates with your vision, and remember: a well-executed launch sets the tone for your book's journey.

Whether you're throwing a party, hosting online, blitzing social media, or blending them all, celebrate the moment—you've worked hard to bring your book to life, and now it's time to share it with the world.

## Hosting a Successful Zoom Book Launch

Hosting a book launch via Zoom is a fantastic way to connect with fans and celebrate your achievement. Although virtual events differ from in-person gatherings, they bring new opportunities—such as affordability, accessibility, and a global reach. Here's a guide to throwing a seamless and exciting Zoom launch.

## Why a Zoom Book Launch?

Virtual book launches have become incredibly popular. While nothing can quite replicate the energy of an in-person gathering, a Zoom launch offers benefits that make it an attractive option:

1. **Reduced Cost**: No need to rent a venue, purchase food, or arrange logistics. Zoom events are budget-friendly, requiring little more than your laptop and an internet connection.
2. **Convenience**: You won't have to haul books or decorations anywhere—just set up from your home, click a button, and start the event.
3. **Expanded Reach**: Anyone with a Zoom link can join, regardless of their location. This makes it easy to connect with friends, family, and fans from all over the world.

## Steps for a Smooth Zoom Launch

### Step 1: Set Up Your Space

Make your background appealing and reflective of your book. Here's how:

- **Create an Eye-Catching Setup:** Place your book on a stand or easel behind you, and consider adding small decorations, like plants or lights.
- **Check Your Lighting:** Good lighting is essential. Position lights in front of or on either side of you to prevent backlighting and shadows.
- **Adjust Your Camera:** Make sure the camera is at eye level to create a more direct, engaging presence.

### Step 2: Invite Everyone Well in Advance

To ensure a strong turnout, start inviting early and continue reminding people as the date approaches:

- **Select Your Date and Time:** Pick a time that works best for your audience—between 5 and 7 p.m. often works well for many time zones.
- **Set Up the Zoom Link:** Schedule your event in Zoom and share the meeting link.
- **Send Invites in Stages:**
  - **Six Weeks Prior:** Send a "Save the Date" with your Zoom link and time.
  - **Weekly Reminders:** In the weeks leading up to the event, send friendly reminders.
  - **Day-of Reminder:** Send a final reminder a few hours before to keep the event top of mind.

## Event Flow and Roles

Running a virtual event is smoother with a little structure. Having a co-host or emcee helps manage the event's flow, allowing you to focus on connecting with guests.

## Key Roles for a Successful Event

- **Emcee:** This person introduces you, guides the event, handles Q&A, and generally keeps things moving.
- **Assistant:** A second helper can monitor the chat, post links to your book, website, and social media, and handle technical issues.

## Planning Your Program

The content of your launch event should be lively and engaging. Here's a suggested structure:

1. **Introduction:** Start with a warm welcome and brief overview of the agenda.
2. **Background on Your Book:** Share your inspiration and writing journey in a few sentences.
3. **Book Reading:** Choose an excerpt that is intriguing yet short (three to five minutes).
4. **Q&A Session:** Open the floor to questions, allowing readers to engage directly.
5. **Call to Action:** Share links to purchase the book and encourage guests to leave a review or follow you on social media.

## Tips for Keeping Engagement High

- **Use Visuals:** Share slides or images related to your book.
- **Encourage Interaction:** Ask guests to post questions or share thoughts in the chat.

- **Include a Raffle or Giveaway:** Keep excitement high by offering a free signed book or book bundle to one lucky attendee.

### Final Touches: Post-Launch Follow-Up

After the event, keep the momentum going:

- **Send a Thank-You Note:** Email attendees with a thank-you message and a link to purchase the book.
- **Share a Recording:** Post a recording on your social media for anyone who missed it.
- **Encourage Reviews:** Politely ask attendees to leave a review on Amazon or Goodreads.

### Emcees, Assistants, and Engagement

A successful virtual event depends heavily on effective hosting and audience engagement, where the role of an emcee, an assistant, and the author's interaction all come together to create an unforgettable experience.

### The Role of the Emcee

The emcee is crucial in ensuring the event runs smoothly, keeping energy high and interactions meaningful. Their primary goal is to keep the spotlight on you, the author, while subtly guiding the flow and making sure all technical aspects are handled.

- **Focus on You, the Author:** The emcee's main job is to spotlight your achievements. They should introduce you and quickly transition the attention to your story, encouraging you to share insights about your journey and book.
- **Engage the Audience:** As the emcee manages the event, they should ask engaging questions, field audience queries, and direct the conversation. This interaction ensures attendees feel part of the celebration and are eager to learn more.

- **Handle the Flow:** They should keep a gentle eye on the clock to ensure a smooth event pace, knowing when to transition from one segment to the next, and gracefully steer the discussion if topics stray.

## The Role of the Assistant

An assistant's role is often more behind the scenes but essential to supporting both you and the emcee. Here's how an assistant can make a big difference:

- **Manage Links and Info in the Chat:** Throughout the event, the assistant should share purchase links, website information, social media tags, or even Venmo/PayPal links if taking direct orders.
- **Encourage Engagement:** The assistant can subtly encourage audience participation by replying to comments or questions in the chat, adding enthusiasm, or thanking guests for attending.
- **Capture the Moment:** Screenshots or virtual photos can add a personal touch to your celebration, and an assistant can handle these tasks so you stay present with your audience.

## Planning Your Program: Key Talking Points

Your virtual launch should be engaging, informative, and personal. Below are key talking points and activities that can help maintain a dynamic program:

- **Welcome and Set the Scene:** Start by welcoming guests, letting them know the agenda, and setting a warm, casual tone.
- **Introduce Your Book:** Share your inspiration behind writing the book, why it matters, and what you hope readers will take away.

- **Share an Excerpt:** Reading a short, impactful passage from your book brings it to life and gives the audience a taste of your style.
- **Audience Q&A:** Allow time for questions from the audience. This part of the event often feels spontaneous and personal, encouraging guests to connect directly with you and your story.
- **Encourage Social Media Sharing:** Ask guests to share their experiences or favorite moments from the event using a unique hashtag to expand your online reach.

## Interactive Ideas to Boost Engagement

Interactive elements keep the energy high and make your event memorable. Here are some ideas to try:

- **Ask for Social Shares:** Encourage attendees to share your book on their social media and leave reviews on platforms like Amazon and Goodreads.
- **Engage Collaborators:** Consider interviewing individuals who played a role in the book's development, like editors, mentors, or friends who inspired specific parts of the story.
- **Run a Giveaway:** For everyone who purchases a book during the event or has already bought one, consider a raffle for a prize. Prizes could include a signed copy of your book, a limited-edition bookmark, or even a personalized note.

## Ending on a High Note: The Big Finish

A memorable wrap-up is the perfect end to your book launch. The emcee should guide a closing celebration that both honors your achievement and makes attendees feel part of the experience.

- **Collect Meaningful Messages:** Ask attendees to drop congratulatory notes in the chat, creating a special keepsake of well-wishes and positivity for you to cherish.

## LAUNCHING YOUR BOOK

- **A Grand Farewell:** As a closing gesture, invite everyone to unmute and offer a round of applause and cheers to celebrate your achievement. This makes for a heartwarming and unforgettable finale.

With a well-organized virtual book launch, an enthusiastic emcee, and interactive moments, you can create a meaningful, accessible, and celebratory experience that resonates with your guests and amplifies your book's reach.

### Adding Energy and Engagement to Your Book Launch Party

Creating an energetic, memorable book launch event can help build buzz for your book. Adding interactive elements like games and challenges is a great way to engage guests and boost social media exposure. Whether your launch is virtual or in person, these activities can make your event more dynamic, encouraging guests to connect with each other—and with your book.

### Icebreakers for an Interactive Launch

Adding a few fun icebreaker activities can help guests feel more relaxed and engaged. Here are two examples to get your party started:

1. Book Party Bingo

Book Party Bingo encourages attendees to learn about your book and engage with each other and with you. Here's how to set it up:

- **Custom Bingo Cards:** Create Bingo cards with squares featuring different tasks related to your book, like "Post a selfie with the book on social media," "Ask the author a question," or "Leave a review on Amazon." You can use online tools to design and print Bingo cards.
- **Instructions for Play:** Explain to guests that completing any row of tasks—vertically, horizontally, or diagonally—earns them a spot in a prize drawing.

- **Prizes:** Reward participants with fun prizes like a signed copy of your book, a gift card, or even a special item inspired by your book's themes.

This game is an excellent way to encourage social media sharing and promote online visibility for your book.

2. **Earn Points for Participation**

Encourage guests to actively participate by awarding points for different actions. Here's how it works:

- **Scorecards:** Create scorecards listing tasks such as "Bring a friend," "Post a photo at the event," "Use the event hashtag," or "Purchase a book." Assign different points for each task to encourage a variety of activities.
- **Tally Up Points:** At the end of the event, have participants submit their points for a chance to win prizes.
- **Prizes:** Offer rewards for the highest scores. These could be anything from merchandise to a private author Q&A or a signed book.

This points-based activity is great for boosting participation and ensuring that everyone feels involved.

## Ways Friends Can Support Your Book Launch

Your friends and family want to help, but they may not know how. Here's a list of ways they can actively support your book's launch—feel free to print this and hand it out at your event or share it on social media:

1. **Purchase Directly:** Ask the author where to purchase the book to maximize royalties.
2. **Share on Social Media:** Post about the book on platforms like Facebook, Instagram, and X. Use relevant hashtags to reach more readers.

3. **Leave a Review**: Reviews on Amazon and Goodreads increase credibility and help future readers decide.
4. **Suggest to Book Clubs**: Recommend the book for local book clubs or group discussions.
5. **Feature in Newsletters**: If they have a newsletter or blog, friends can feature your book to reach a wider audience.
6. **Video Review**: Record a video review to share on social media and link to the book's page.
7. **Library Requests**: Ask local libraries to carry the book; libraries pay attention to patron requests.
8. **Gift the Book**: Buy additional copies as gifts, helping introduce your book to more readers.
9. **Share on Pinterest**: Create a Pinterest post linking to your Amazon page, showcasing your book cover or any themed images.
10. **Tweet and Retweet**: Tweet about the book and retweet your posts to increase exposure.
11. **Promote at Events**: Suggest the author as a speaker or guest at events, Rotary clubs, or other organizations.
12. **Join Author Events**: Attend or share the author's launch party or book signing events to add to the excitement.

Adding these interactive, fun, and promotional strategies can turn your book launch into a memorable event that generates buzz, connects you with your audience, and builds momentum for your book's journey in the world. Whether using Bingo cards, point-based challenges, or friend and family support, these tools can help ensure your launch party is impactful and inspiring.

# CHAPTER 9

# YOUR BOOK IS LIVE—NOW WHAT?

Congratulations! Your book is officially published and available to readers worldwide. But before you sit back and relax, there are some crucial next steps to help boost your book's visibility and optimize your sales. Here's your post-launch action plan to ensure your book hits the ground running.

**First Things First: Update Your Email Signature**

This might seem like a small step, but it's an easy way to promote your book with every email you send. Simply add a line to your signature, such as:

"Author of [Your Book Title] – Now Available on Amazon!"

Include a direct link to your Amazon sales page so recipients can easily check it out. This is a low-effort, consistent way to reach your contacts and increase exposure.

**Register Your Book with the Library of Congress**

While registering with the Library of Congress (LOC) isn't mandatory, it's a good practice that can offer additional credibility. Here's how to get started:

1. **Visit the Registration Page**: Go to www.copyright.gov/registration/literary-works.
2. **Select Form TX**: Click on "Literary Work (Form TX)" to begin the process. This form covers books, manuscripts, and literary content.
3. **Watch the Tutorial**: There's a video on the page that guides you through filling out the form.
4. **Pay the Fee**: The current fee for registration is $65 (at the time of writing).
5. **Act Quickly**: You have ninety days from your book's publication date to complete this process.

Registering your book protects your copyright and ensures that it's officially cataloged for future reference.

**Optimize Your Amazon Sales Page**

Your Amazon sales page is your primary storefront. Think of it as your book's first impression. Here are five steps to make sure it's optimized for maximum visibility and conversions.

1. Use Effective Keywords

Amazon is the top search engine for products. Keywords help potential readers find your book among millions of listings. When setting up your Kindle Direct Publishing (KDP) account, you can choose up to **seven keywords**. Make them count by selecting terms relevant to your genre, topic, and reader interests.

- **Research Tools**: Use resources like Publisher Rocket to find high-performing keywords that your target audience is searching for. Publisher Rocket offers insights on keyword competition, search volume, and potential book categories.

2. Choose the Right Categories

Amazon's **browse categories** differ from the initial category choices you make in KDP. These allow you to target niche topics where your book is more likely to stand out.

- **How to Update Categories**:
    o Log into your KDP account.
    o Scroll to the bottom of the page and click on "Contact Us."
    o Select "Amazon Product Page and Expanded Distribution" and then "Update Amazon Categories."
    o Use Publisher Rocket or explore Amazon's category list manually to find the best fit.

Selecting specific categories with less competition gives your book a better chance of hitting the bestseller lists.

3. Enable the "Look Inside" Feature

The **Look Inside** feature is a preview tool that lets potential readers sample the first few pages of your book. This feature is automatically activated within four days of publishing via KDP. If it doesn't show up, contact KDP support for assistance.

Providing a preview of your book increases engagement and can help convince readers to make a purchase.

4. Format Your Product Description

Your product description is the sales pitch for your book. KDP requires it to be formatted in **HTML**, which can be challenging if you're not tech-savvy.

- **Tip:** Use Kindlepreneur's free HTML Book Description Generator to easily format your text with bold, italics, and bullet points, making your description more readable and visually appealing.

5. Set Up Your Amazon Author Central Page

Your Amazon Author Central page is like your author profile on Amazon. It provides readers with more information about you and links to all your books.

- **How to Set It Up:**
    - Go to amazon.authorcentral.com.
    - Log in using your KDP account credentials.
    - Add your author photo, bio, blog feed, and any editorial reviews.
    - Keep this page updated with new releases, videos, and events.

Having an Author Central page helps build your author brand and gives readers a place to learn more about you and your work.

## Promote Your Book: Leverage Social Media and Reviews

Your book launch isn't just a one-day event—it's a continuous process. Use social media, email marketing, and reader engagement strategies to keep the momentum going.

1. **Social Media Blitz:** Share your book's release on platforms like Instagram, X, and Facebook. Use engaging visuals and direct links to your Amazon page.
2. **Encourage Reviews:** Reviews are critical for building credibility. Ask your readers to leave honest reviews on Amazon and Goodreads.
3. **Utilize Your Email List:** Send an email to your subscribers announcing the launch. Offer a special discount or a bonus gift for early buyers.

## Planning Your Virtual Book Tour

A **virtual book tour** is an excellent way to market your book without physically traveling. Instead of visiting bookstores, you "tour" different blogs, podcasts, and social media platforms, sharing your book with diverse audiences. The goal is to make your book visible everywhere your target readers might be.

## Why a Virtual Book Tour?

- **Wider Reach:** You can connect with readers across the globe without leaving your home.
- **Cost-Effective:** It eliminates travel expenses, making it budget-friendly.
- **Targeted Exposure:** You can tailor your stops to blogs and podcasts that align with your book's genre and audience.

## How to Plan a Successful Virtual Book Tour

1. **Research and Select the Right Blogs/Podcasts:**
    - Identify blogs and podcasts in your genre that have a strong following.
    - Look for platforms that feature book reviews, author interviews, and guest posts.

2. **Organize the Tour Schedule:**
   o Aim for two to three stops per week over a four-to-six-week period for maximum impact.
   o Create a detailed calendar outlining which blogs or podcasts you will visit each day.
3. **Prepare Your Content:**
   o Write guest posts, provide exclusive excerpts, and prepare a Q&A.
   o Make sure your content is engaging and tailored to the audience of each platform.
4. **Promote Each Stop:**
   o Share every tour stop on your social media channels.
   o Encourage followers to visit the blogs and podcasts, comment, and share the posts.
5. **Consider Hiring a Professional Tour Organizer:**
   o If you don't have time to coordinate the tour, hire a virtual book tour service. They have established relationships with bloggers and can streamline the process.

### Tools for a Virtual Book Tour

- **Book Bloggers Directory**: Find a list of reputable book bloggers.
- **Google Alerts**: Set up alerts for your book title to track mentions during the tour.
- **Canva**: Create eye-catching visuals for each stop of the tour.

### Optimizing Your Goodreads Author Account

Goodreads is a social media platform for book lovers, making it a powerful tool for authors to connect with readers and build buzz. If you haven't already, it's time to set up your **Goodreads Author Account** and optimize it to showcase your book.

## YOUR BOOK IS LIVE—NOW WHAT?

### Steps to Set Up and Optimize Your Goodreads Author Page

1. **Fill Out Your Bio Completely:**
   - Write an engaging bio that tells readers about your background and why you wrote your book.
   - Add a professional author photo that reflects your brand.

2. **Add Your Book to the Catalog:**
   - Make sure your book is listed on Goodreads and linked to your author profile.
   - Include all relevant details like the book description, cover image, and publication date.

3. **Create Discussion Questions:**
   - Write a set of discussion questions for book clubs. This helps readers engage with your book and sparks deeper conversations.

4. **Join Goodreads Lists:**
   - Find curated lists that fit your book's genre and themes. Adding your book to these lists can increase its visibility among readers who enjoy similar titles.

5. **Share Excerpts and Book Trailers:**
   - Post short excerpts or a book trailer video to give potential readers a taste of your book.

6. **Import Your Blog:**
   - Sync your author blog with Goodreads so your latest posts appear on your author page. This helps keep your profile active and engaging.

### Tips for Engaging on Goodreads

- **Answer Reader Questions:** Engage with readers by responding to their questions about your book.

- **Host a Q&A Session:** Plan a live Q&A session on Goodreads to interact with readers and build excitement for your book.

## Organize a Goodreads Giveaway

A **Goodreads Giveaway** is a powerful marketing tool that puts your book in front of thousands of potential readers. Those who don't win a copy often add it to their "Want to Read" shelf, increasing your book's visibility.

### Benefits of a Goodreads Giveaway

- **Boosts Visibility:** Your book will appear on the giveaway page, which is browsed by millions of readers.
- **Increases "Want to Read" Adds:** Readers who don't win often add your book to their reading lists, which can lead to future purchases.
- **Encourages Reviews:** Winners are prompted to leave reviews, which helps build credibility and attract more readers.

### How to Run a Successful Goodreads Giveaway

1. **Choose Your Giveaway Type:**
    - Offer one hundred eBook copies for maximum exposure. eBooks are cost-effective and easy to distribute.
2. **Set the Campaign Duration:**
    - A one-month campaign tends to work best, giving readers enough time to discover and enter the giveaway.
3. **Plan the Timing:**
    - Start your giveaway mid-month to avoid competition from the typical first-through-thirtieth giveaway period.

4. **Promote Your Giveaway:**
    - Share the giveaway on your social media platforms and email newsletter to increase participation.
5. **Leverage Goodreads' Follow-Up:**
    - Goodreads will send reminders to winners, encouraging them to rate and review your book.

## Current Pricing for Goodreads Giveaways

As of this writing, the cost to run a Goodreads Giveaway is $119. This fee covers the entire process, including promotion and distribution.

## Podcasting, Profile Optimization, and Book Promotion Sites

Podcasting has become one of the hottest ways for authors to connect with readers and reach new audiences. Coupled with optimizing your Amazon Public Profile and leveraging high-quality book promotion websites, you can amplify your marketing efforts and make your book stand out.

## Why Podcasting is a Game-Changer

Appearing as a guest on podcasts is an exceptional way to market your book. Unlike traditional advertising, podcasts give you a platform to engage with a dedicated audience interested in your genre or topic. By sharing your expertise and discussing your book, you can captivate listeners who are likely to become new readers.

## Benefits of Being a Podcast Guest:

1. **Long-Lasting Exposure:** Podcasts are evergreen content; once your episode is live, it stays online indefinitely, continuing to reach new listeners over time.
2. **Targeted Audience:** Podcast hosts often have a loyal following, and you can tap into this established audience to boost your book's visibility.

3. **SEO Boost**: Many podcasts have show notes and links to your book, which helps improve your search engine ranking.

## How to Find Podcasts

- **Matchmaker.fm**: Connect with podcast hosts looking for guests.
- **Podcastguests.com**: List your profile and get matched with relevant shows.
- **Podmatch.com**: A matchmaking service for podcast guests and hosts.

You can also search manually by Googling "best podcasts for [your target audience]" to find shows that fit your niche.

## Creating an Effective Podcast One-Sheet

A podcast one-sheet is a promotional tool designed to pitch yourself as a guest to podcast hosts. It's a concise document that highlights your expertise, the value you can bring to the podcast, and your contact information.

## What to Include:

1. **Introduction**: A brief, engaging overview of who you are and your background.
2. **Talking Points**: List three to five topics or questions you can discuss that are tailored to the podcast's audience.
3. **Book Information**: Include a brief description of your book, notable reviews, or awards.
4. **Social Proof**: Mention other podcasts you've been featured on (if applicable).
5. **Contact Details**: Provide your email, social media handles, and website link.

A well-crafted one-sheet increases your chances of being invited as a guest and makes it easier for hosts to see the value you'll bring to their audience.

## Optimizing Your Amazon Public Profile

Your Amazon Public Profile is different from your Author Central page and can be a powerful marketing tool when used effectively. This profile appears whenever you leave a review on Amazon, helping to increase your visibility.

**Steps to Optimize Your Amazon Public Profile:**

1. **Log In:**
   - Access your profile through your regular Amazon account (not Author Central).
2. **Edit Your Profile:**
   - Click on "Your Public Profile" under the Personalization section.
3. **Add a Professional Headshot:**
   - Choose a clear, friendly photo that aligns with your author brand.
4. **Create a Short Bio:**
   - Write a seventy-five-word bio that includes keywords relevant to your book's genre or subject matter.
5. **Include a Signature Line:**
   - Add a line that links to your website or Amazon author page (only in the designated link section).
6. **Utilize Keywords:**
   - Incorporate relevant keywords to help improve your profile's visibility in search results.

By optimizing this profile, you can subtly market your book every time you engage on Amazon.

## Top Book Promotion Websites

Promoting your book on reputable websites is a great way to boost your online presence, drive traffic, and increase sales. Here are some top sites where you can list your book for free, providing valuable backlinks and additional exposure.

## Recommended Book Promotion Sites

1. **BookBub:** A popular platform for book recommendations and promotions. You can create an author profile and list your book.
2. **HometownReads.com:** A site that connects local authors with local readers.
3. **Awesomegang.com:** Provides author interviews and a platform to showcase your book.
4. **MyBookPlace.net:** Features book listings and author interviews.
5. **LibraryThing.com:** Connect with readers and list your book in the catalog.
6. **AuthorsDen.com:** A community site for authors to share their work and connect with readers.

These platforms help increase your book's visibility and improve your search engine rankings through quality backlinks.

## Author Services for Additional Support

There are numerous author services available to assist with marketing, reviews, and promotional efforts. These services can be invaluable if you want to outsource some of the more time-consuming tasks.

## Top Author Services:

- **ChoosyBookworm.com:** Helps authors connect with readers and offers promotional opportunities.

- **IndiesUnlimited.com:** Provides marketing tips and promotional services for independent authors.
- **FeatheredQuill.com:** Offers book reviews and publicity services.

Choose a service that aligns with your marketing budget and target audience. Many of these platforms offer a range of packages, so you can find one that fits your specific needs.

# CHAPTER 10

## LEVERAGING REVIEWS AND COMMUNITY SUPPORT

Getting reviews is crucial for boosting your book's visibility, credibility, and sales potential. While many authors focus heavily on prelaunch reviews, securing reviews throughout your book's first year is equally important. Here's a comprehensive strategy to help you garner valuable feedback, build momentum, and leverage reviews for greater success.

**The Power of Book Reviews**

Reviews are one of the most effective forms of social proof for your book. They influence purchasing decisions, improve your search ranking on Amazon, and can even catch the eye of traditional publishers scouting for successful self-published works.

**Why Reviews Matter:**

1. **Enhanced Visibility:** More reviews help boost your book's ranking in Amazon's search algorithm, making it easier for potential readers to discover your book.
2. **Social Proof:** Positive reviews increase trust and credibility, making readers more likely to buy your book.
3. **Publisher Interest:** High review counts can demonstrate strong reader interest, attracting attention from traditional publishers looking for promising titles.

**Review Milestones:**

Aim for the following milestones to increase your chances of success on Amazon:

- **Twenty-Five Reviews:** A good starting point for building initial credibility.
- **Seventy-Five Reviews:** A strong signal to the Amazon algorithm that your book is gaining traction.
- **One hundred-plus Reviews:** Establishes your book as a popular, well-liked choice in its genre.

Set a goal to reach **150 reviews within the first four months** after launch. It's ambitious, but it can significantly increase your book's visibility and sales.

**Free Book Review Sites**

There are numerous reputable websites where you can submit your book for free reviews. These platforms can help you gather authentic feedback without breaking your marketing budget. However, keep in mind that competition is fierce, and getting a review isn't guaranteed. Submitting consistently, with a professionally edited manuscript and eye-catching cover, can improve your chances.

## LEVERAGING REVIEWS AND COMMUNITY SUPPORT

Top Free Book Review Sites:

1. **ReadersFavorite.com**: Offers free reviews and is well-regarded for its professional feedback.
2. **MidwestBookReview.com**: A popular choice for indie authors seeking credibility.
3. **Booklife.com** (Publishers Weekly indie arm): Connects self-published authors with potential reviewers.
4. **SanFranciscoBookReview.com**: Known for its wide reader base and diverse review categories.
5. **TheIndieView.com**: Lists numerous reviewers who are open to indie submissions.
6. **Reedsy Blog Reviewers**: A comprehensive list of book review blogs curated by Reedsy.
7. **TheNewBookReview.blogspot.com**: Offers a platform for authors to share reviews and gain visibility.

**TIP**: Aim to submit your book to at least **five review sites per week** during the first two months post-launch.

Leveraging Social Media for Reviews

Facebook groups, Instagram bookstagrammers, and Goodreads communities are fantastic places to connect with readers willing to review your book. When reaching out, be respectful, personal, and clear about what you're requesting.

How to Approach Reviewers:

1. **Personalize Your Message**: Mention why you think they'll enjoy your book based on their previous reviews.
2. **Provide Multiple Formats**: Offer your book in different formats (PDF, ePub, Kindle) to accommodate reviewers' preferences.
3. **Set Clear Expectations**: Let them know you're looking for an honest review in exchange for a free copy.

Top Social Media Groups for Book Reviews:

- **Facebook Groups**: Look for groups like "Book Review Central" or "Indie Author Book Reviews."
- **Instagram**: Use hashtags like #bookreviewer, #bookstagram, and #ARCreader to find reviewers.
- **Goodreads Communities**: Join genre-specific groups and connect with members interested in reviewing.

## Paid Book Review Options

While there's an ongoing debate about whether or not to pay for reviews, reputable paid review services offer honest feedback, not guaranteed positive reviews. These services often have extensive networks and can help your book reach a wider audience.

Top Paid Review Services:

1. **Kirkus Indie Reviews**: Known for its thorough and respected reviews. It's a costly option but has significant credibility.
2. **BlueInk Review**: Specializes in indie and self-published books, providing professional and detailed feedback.
3. **BookLife Reviews**: Offers honest, in-depth reviews and distributes them to industry professionals.

**TIP**: Paid reviews can range from $300 to $600, so factor this into your marketing budget.

## How to Use Your Reviews Effectively

Once you receive your editorial reviews, it's important to strategically leverage them across your marketing channels to maximize impact.

1. **Add to Your Book Cover**: If you receive a glowing endorsement from a reputable source, consider adding it to your book cover. A strong quote from a well-known

reviewer can be featured on the front or back cover for added credibility.

2. **Update Your Amazon Author Central Page:** Include your editorial reviews on your Amazon Author Central page. This not only enhances your author profile but also boosts the visibility of your book on Amazon's platform.

3. **Feature in Your Marketing Materials:** Use excerpts from your reviews in your press releases, email newsletters, and social media posts. Highlight the most impactful quotes to attract new readers.

4. **Share on Social Media:** Turn your reviews into eye-catching graphics using tools like Canva. Share these graphics on Instagram, Facebook, LinkedIn, and X to generate buzz and engagement.

5. **Create a Testimonials Page on Your Website:** Dedicate a section of your author website to showcase your best reviews. This serves as a hub for readers, media, and industry professionals to see the positive reception your book has received.

6. **Include in Promotional Flyers and Postcards:** If you're attending book signings or events, include your top reviews on promotional materials like flyers, bookmarks, and postcards. This adds an extra layer of credibility when engaging with potential readers.

7. **Highlight in Press Releases:** Feature your most compelling reviews in your press releases. Quotes from respected sources can increase the likelihood of your book being covered by media outlets.

TIP: Keep a document with all your favorite review quotes. It's a handy resource when creating new marketing content.

## Building a Review Request System

To streamline your efforts, create a simple review request system that you can use to consistently gather feedback.

## How to Build Your System:

1. **Create a Standard Email Template**: Write a friendly, professional email requesting a review and explaining how it benefits both the reader and the author.
2. **Offer an Incentive**: While you can't pay for reviews, you can offer something of value, like a free chapter or entry into a giveaway, as a thank-you gesture.
3. **Follow Up**: Politely follow up with reviewers who haven't responded after a week or two. Sometimes a gentle reminder is all it takes.

## Example Review Request Email:

*Subject: Your Feedback on [Book Title] Would Mean the World!*

Dear [Reviewer's Name],

I hope you're doing well! I wanted to reach out because I thought you might enjoy my new book, [Book Title]. If you're interested, I'd love to send you a free copy in exchange for an honest review on Amazon or Goodreads.

Your feedback helps other readers discover the book and means so much to me as an author.

Thank you in advance for considering it, and I'm looking forward to hearing your thoughts!

Warm regards,
[Your Name]

## Navigating Media Outreach for Authors

Media outreach is a crucial component of your book marketing plan. It's all about connecting with the right outlets that can amplify your message to your target audience. While landing a feature in a national publication or on a top-rated show can be transformative, don't overlook smaller, niche media opportunities.

These can be equally impactful, especially for reaching a specific audience that's genuinely interested in your book's topic.

## Why Media Outreach Matters

Media outreach helps build credibility and enhances visibility for your book. By strategically pitching to various media outlets, you can reach potential readers who might otherwise never hear about your book. The goal is not only to promote but to engage with your audience by offering valuable insights related to your book's theme.

## Tapping Into Niche Media Outlets

Remember, every hobby, interest, or industry has its own set of publications, blogs, and forums. Your job is to find these specific outlets and pitch your book or expertise in a way that resonates with their audience. For instance:

- **Neighborhood Newspapers**: Local papers may be more open to featuring an author from the community.
- **Industry Newsletters**: These are targeted to specific professional groups, making them ideal for nonfiction authors.
- **Specialty Magazines**: If your book covers a niche topic, like gardening or travel, look for specialty publications that cater to those interests.

## Making Waves on Radio

Radio remains a powerful medium for author interviews, and it's more accessible than ever, thanks to online radio and podcasts.

1. **Register with Guest Services**: Create a profile on platforms like Radio Guest List, which connects authors with shows seeking expert guests.
2. **Explore Radio Blogs**: Use sites like BlogTalkRadio to find genre-specific radio shows.

3. **Craft Your Pitch Carefully**: When reaching out to radio producers, pitch an engaging topic rather than your book. Make it clear why your story would appeal to their audience.

**Tip**: If you're booked for an interview, provide the host with a list of suggested questions. This helps steer the conversation and ensures they mention your book and website multiple times.

### Taking Your Pitch to TV

Local TV shows, especially morning programs, often look for content featuring local authors or community stories.

- **Research Local Programming**: Start with shows that highlight events or community news. Tailor your pitch to suggest a segment that fits their format.
- **Focus on the Story, Not the Sale**: When pitching to TV, frame your segment idea around the broader story or theme of your book, not just the book itself.

**Example**: If your book is about overcoming adversity, pitch a story related to resilience, timed around Mental Health Awareness Month.

### Newspaper Outreach

Local newspapers are often overlooked, but they can be powerful allies in your media strategy.

1. **Target City, County, and State Papers**: These publications frequently feature local authors, especially if your book has a regional connection.
2. **Look for Community Features**: Reach out to editors who handle community stories or lifestyle features. A well-crafted pitch about your book's theme can land you a valuable spot.

## Exploring Newsletters

Don't underestimate the impact of newsletters, which can deliver your message directly to a curated list of readers.

- **Alumni Newsletters**: Your college or university alumni network may feature your book in their publication.
- **Professional Organizations**: Industry-related newsletters are great for nonfiction authors looking to reach a specific demographic.
- **Company Newsletters**: If you have a corporate background, see if your company's newsletter can feature your book.

**Tip**: When submitting for a feature, provide a short bio, book cover image, and a link to your Amazon page or author website.

## Tips for Crafting a Successful Media Pitch

Pitching to the media requires a strategic approach. Here's how to make your pitch stand out:

1. **Pitch the Story, Not the Book**: Frame your pitch around an engaging story or theme related to your book rather than focusing solely on the book itself.
2. **Keep It Concise**: Busy producers and editors don't have time for lengthy emails. Keep your pitch short and to the point—no more than one page.
3. **Highlight Your Hook**: Lead with a compelling hook—a short sentence that grabs attention. Explain why your topic is relevant and timely.
4. **Use Bullet Points**: Format your email for easy reading. Use bullet points to outline the key points of your pitch quickly.
5. **Be Ready When They Are**: If a producer shows interest, respond promptly. Media operates on tight deadlines, and delays could mean missed opportunities.

### Hidden Gem: Become an Expert Commenter

Engaging in the comment sections of popular articles, blog posts, and forums is a subtle but effective way to establish your expertise. By sharing thoughtful, relevant insights, you can attract attention without directly pitching your book.

- **Join Online Discussions**: Engage in discussions on Quora or relevant blog posts. Offer valuable input based on your book's theme.
- **Focus on Value, Not Promotion**: Instead of blatantly promoting your book, provide helpful comments that demonstrate your knowledge. Readers who find your insights useful will often seek out your book on their own.

### Becoming a Great Interview Guest

Landing a media interview can be a significant boost for your book's promotion, but the real challenge lies in nailing that interview. Being a memorable guest requires preparation, clear messaging, and a few strategic tips to keep in mind.

### Be Prepared

Preparation is your foundation. Know your book inside out, including its key themes, unique aspects, and any background stories that might interest the audience. You should be able to speak fluently and confidently about your topic, even if the conversation veers off script.

**Tip**: Research the show or podcast before the interview. Familiarize yourself with the host's style, the typical format, and the kind of topics usually discussed. This knowledge allows you to tailor your responses to fit the show's vibe.

### Know Your Talking Points

While it's essential to be conversational, having a set of three to five clear talking points will help keep you focused. Think of these as the core messages you want to convey about your book and its importance. These points should be engaging and tie back to the central theme of your book.

**Example**: If your book is a memoir about overcoming adversity, your talking points might include the emotional journey of writing it, key lessons learned, and how it can help readers facing similar challenges.

### It's About the Story, Not Just the Book

Remember, it's not the host's job to sell your book. Their audience tunes in for compelling stories and valuable information. So, focus on storytelling. Share personal anecdotes, the "why" behind your book, and any unique experiences related to its creation. The more relatable and engaging your narrative, the more likely listeners will be interested in purchasing your book.

### Offer a Giveaway

Consider asking the producer if you can offer a giveaway during the interview. This could be a free signed copy of your book, an exclusive chapter, or any bonus content that could entice the audience. A giveaway helps generate excitement and provides a clear call to action.

**Tip**: Make sure the giveaway is easy for listeners to enter. Direct them to your website or social media for participation, increasing engagement and visibility.

### Provide Essential Information

Ensure the host has all the necessary details about you and your book. This includes your website, social media handles, and the book's title. While it's not their primary role to promote your book, most hosts will be gracious enough to mention it if you provide the information upfront.

**Example:** Before the interview, send the host a one-page info sheet with your bio, book summary, website link, and social media handles.

### Follow Up with Gratitude

After the interview, show your appreciation with a handwritten thank-you note. While emails are convenient, a handwritten card stands out and leaves a lasting impression. It shows that you value the opportunity and builds goodwill for potential future collaborations.

### Pro Tip: Craft a Winning Media Kit

To make your media outreach more effective, create a professional media kit. This document should include your author bio, book cover, press release, sample interview questions, and contact information. It's a helpful resource for producers and hosts, making it easier for them to promote you effectively.

### Maximizing Article Exposure

Writing articles on your book's topic can further extend your reach and boost your authority. Platforms like **Medium.com** offer a space for you to publish articles that can link back to your book's sales page or your author website. These articles can help establish your expertise and keep your content circulating online.

**Tip:** Aim for articles that offer valuable insights rather than a hard sell. Readers are more likely to check out your book if they feel you've provided useful information.

### Paid Advertising: Google and Facebook Ads

While organic promotion is effective, paid advertising can accelerate your reach. A Google Ads campaign can place your book in front of readers who are actively searching for similar topics. It's a powerful tool if you're targeting a niche market.

- **Google Ads**: Focus on high-intent keywords related to your book's genre or theme. David Rothwell's **ROI Protected™ system** offers a profit-driven approach, ensuring you only pay for profitable clicks.
- **Facebook Ads**: Facebook allows for targeted ad campaigns, enabling you to reach readers who match your ideal demographic. Dave Chesson's **Kindlepreneur** offers valuable resources on creating effective Facebook ads for book promotion.

**Pro Tip:** Use **Publisher Rocket** to find the best keywords and categories for your Amazon ads. It's a one-time investment that can pay off significantly if you're planning multiple ad campaigns.

**Leverage Your Network for In-Home Book Parties**

Ask your friends and connections if they'd consider hosting an informal book party at their home. This type of event is similar to a book club but focuses on showcasing your book and creating an intimate setting for discussion. It's a great way to connect directly with potential readers, answer their questions, and leave them excited about your book.

**Tip:** Bring copies of your book to sell at the event and offer to sign them for attendees. Personal touches like this make the experience memorable and boost your book sales.

# CHAPTER 11

## MARKETING YOUR BOOK

Social media platforms like Pinterest offer unique promotional opportunities, and book clubs remain an effective way to engage readers. Let's dive into strategies for making the most of both.

**Promoting Your Book on Pinterest**

Pinterest is not just a digital pinboard; it's a powerful visual search engine. It's an excellent platform for authors to share creative content and attract new readers, especially if your target audience includes women in their thirties to fifties who enjoy discovering new books and ideas.

1. Create Engaging Boards

Organize boards that reflect your book's themes and genre. For instance:

- **Nonfiction Authors**: Create boards for leadership tips, writing advice, or your favorite book recommendations.
- **Fiction Authors**: Design boards dedicated to your book's characters, settings, or themes. Create a mood board that captures the atmosphere of your story.

The goal is to curate content that resonates with your ideal readers and provides value.

2. Use Keywords in Descriptions

When you pin images or quotes from your book, use relevant keywords in the description. For example, if you wrote a historical romance, include tags like #HistoricalRomance or #LoveStory. These tags help your pins appear in search results, attracting readers who are already looking for similar content.

3. Promote Giveaways and Lead Magnets

Pinterest is great for generating leads. Design a pin that advertises a free eBook chapter or an exclusive checklist related to your book's topic. Link this pin to a landing page on your website where readers can sign up to receive the free content, helping you build your email list.

4. Create Eye-Catching Graphics

Design quotes, excerpts, or character illustrations using Canva or PicMonkey. Be sure to add your book title and author name to each graphic. Sharing these visuals on Pinterest not only increases visibility but also helps with branding.

**Pro Tip**: Create infographics, such as "Top 10 Must-Read Books in [Your Genre]," and include your book on the list. Infographics are highly shareable and attract more engagement.

## MARKETING YOUR BOOK

5. **Engage Consistently**

Pinterest rewards activity. Aim to pin consistently, around twenty to twenty-five pins a day. Use a mix of your own content and repins from other users. This shows you're active on the platform and can help build your following faster.

6. **Utilize Group Boards**

Join and contribute to group boards in your genre. This expands your reach instantly, as group boards have multiple contributors and a wider audience. Your pins will be seen by more people, increasing the likelihood of engagement.

### Connecting with Book Clubs

Book clubs are a fantastic way to connect with passionate readers who can become your biggest advocates. Let's explore how to effectively market to book clubs.

1. **Create a Book Club Page on Your Website**

Dedicate a section of your website specifically for book clubs. Include discussion guides, suggested questions, and a contact form for clubs interested in having you as a guest—either in person or via Zoom.

2. **Engage with Book Club Members**

Encourage your readers to recommend your book to their clubs. Offer to join their meetings for a Q&A session or reading. This personal touch can leave a lasting impression and lead to more word-of-mouth recommendations.

3. **Utilize Goodreads and LibraryThing**

Set up a profile on Goodreads and LibraryThing. These platforms are where readers gather to share reviews and book recommendations. Mention in your profile that you're open to book club invitations and include a link to your book club discussion guide.

4. Partner with Local Libraries

Reach out to libraries in your area and offer your book for their book club programs. Many libraries host regular book club meetings and are always on the lookout for new titles to feature. This is a great way to gain exposure and connect with readers directly.

5. Create Promotional Materials

Design postcards, flyers, or bookmarks that specifically advertise your willingness to visit book clubs. Include these in every book you sell, hand them out at author events, and leave them at local bookstores and libraries.

**Strategies for Hosting a Book Club Event**

Organizing an event for book clubs can be a great way to boost engagement. Here's how to plan an effective session:

1. **Prepare Discussion Questions**

Provide thought-provoking questions related to your book's themes. This will make the conversation more dynamic and offer readers deeper insights into the story.

2. **Offer Signed Copies**

Bring a few signed copies as giveaways or door prizes. Personalized, signed books make for memorable gifts and create a stronger connection with readers.

## 3. Share Behind-the-Scenes Stories

Readers love getting a peek behind the curtain. Share anecdotes about the writing process, challenges you faced while creating your characters, or any interesting research tidbits.

## Final Tips for Book Club Marketing

- **Use Social Media:** Post photos from book club meetings on your social media accounts and tag the clubs. This shows you're active and engaged with your readers.
- **Collaborate with Other Authors:** Partner with fellow authors to create a book bundle or host joint book club events. This can expand your reach to new audiences.
- **Keep It Fun:** Consider organizing a themed event related to your book. If your story is set in Paris, host a Parisian-themed book club night with French snacks and drinks.

## Unique Book Marketing Strategies for Your Self-Published Title

Effective book promotion goes beyond traditional marketing methods. Let's dive into some innovative strategies to get your book noticed, including creative merchandise and leveraging book contests.

## Creative Merchandise for Book Promotion

Creating fun, branded products tied to your book is an excellent way to generate buzz and start conversations. Here are some options to consider:

## 1. Customized PopSockets and Phone Cases

Design a PopSocket or phone case with your book cover. These small accessories are eye-catching and make fantastic giveaways. Use websites like PopSockets Custom Shop or CafePress to create your designs.

**Why This Works:** Every time someone uses their phone, they're showing off your book, acting as a mini billboard.

2. **Personalized Stamps and Decals**

Create custom stamps or stickers featuring your book cover or a memorable quote. Zazzle offers a variety of options for personalized products. These items are perfect for signing events, and readers can use the decals on their laptops or noteBooks.

**Pro Tip:** Choose a short, impactful quote from your book to include on the decals. This makes them more engaging and memorable.

3. **Branded Merchandise**

Put your book's imagery or key messages on everyday items like mugs, noteBooks, t-shirts, tote bags, and even luggage tags. Websites like Zazzle make it easy to create and order these products. Consider using these items as incentives for social media contests or special pre-order bonuses.

**Engagement Tip:** Run a contest where readers post photos of themselves using the merchandise with a dedicated hashtag. This increases visibility and encourages reader interaction.

### Entering Book Contests: A Strategy for Building Credibility

Book contests are a fantastic way to gain recognition and credibility, especially for self-published authors. Winning or even becoming a finalist can boost your book's visibility and give it a badge of honor that appeals to readers and booksellers alike.

1. **Choose the Right Contests**

There are countless book awards out there, each with its own focus and audience. Here's a short list of reputable contests to consider:

# MARKETING YOUR BOOK

- **IPPY Book Awards:** Celebrates independent and self-published titles. Winners receive substantial media exposure.
- **Writer's Digest Self-Published Book Awards:** One of the most prestigious awards for indie authors, offering a cash prize and industry recognition.
- **Reader's Favorite Book Awards:** Known for their detailed, honest reviews and a wide range of genre categories.
- **Foreword INDIES Book Awards:** A great choice for reaching libraries and indie booksellers.
- **Nautilus Book Awards:** Focuses on books that inspire and promote positive change in the world.

**Research Tip:** Check contest deadlines, as most are based on the year of publication. If your book is releasing late in the year, consider listing the copyright for the upcoming year.

2. Budget and Entry Tips

Most contests charge entry fees ranging from $50 to $100 and require a few copies of your book. Here's how to make the most of your investment:

- **Plan Your Budget:** Enter three to five contests to maximize your chances without overspending.
- **Targeted Contests:** Look for specialized contests (e.g., children's books, romance, cookbooks) that align with your genre.

**Caution:** Be wary of scams. Do thorough research on the contest's reputation before submitting your entry.

## What to Do When You Win an Award

Winning a book award is an incredible milestone that can significantly elevate your marketing efforts. Here's how to leverage your win for maximum impact:

1. Update All Your Author Branding

Include "Award-Winning Author" in your email signature, business cards, and website. This adds an extra layer of credibility and signals quality to potential readers.

**Branding Tip:** Update your Amazon Author Central page and social media profiles with the new title.

2. Revamp Your Book's Marketing Materials

Add the award seal to your book cover, bookmarks, and any promotional materials. This visual cue immediately grabs attention and enhances your book's appeal.

**Marketing Tip:** If you're updating your book cover, use this opportunity to gather new buzz and relaunch your book with the award prominently displayed.

3. Send Out Press Releases

Let the media know about your achievement. A press release can help generate additional coverage, especially with local newspapers, industry blogs, and genre-specific publications.

**Pro Tip:** Include photos of you holding the award. It's a great way to add a personal touch and make your win more relatable.

**Bookstores: Should You Pursue Them?**

Bookstores might seem like an obvious place to market your book, but they often aren't the best option, especially for self-published authors. Most traditional bookstores expect a **40 percent discount** on your book, and if your book doesn't sell within ninety days, they might ship it back—at your expense. Even with a distributor, the discount can climb to **55–65 percent**, making profitability challenging.

## Local Independent Bookstores: The Exception

Local independent bookstores are community hubs and may offer more support for new authors. They often allow consignment sales, which means they'll display your book and only charge a fee if it sells. Here's how to approach them:

1. **Contact the Acquisitions Manager:** Ask if they're willing to stock your book. Bring a copy and pitch why it will resonate with their customers.
2. **Support Them in Return:** Encourage your friends and followers to purchase from these stores. If your book performs well, they might feature it on a **Spotlight Table**, giving it more visibility.

## Book Signings: A Risky Investment

A traditional book signing sounds exciting, but the reality is that they often don't yield great results unless you already have a substantial fan base. On average, only about **five books** are sold per event, and with the bookstore taking a cut of around **40 percent,** your profits can be minimal. It's a time-consuming endeavor that doesn't always pay off.

## Alternatives: Why Book Readings Are Better

Instead of book signings, focus on **book readings**. They're more engaging and allow for deeper interaction with potential readers. During a reading, you can create a connection with the audience, which is a key component of effective book marketing.

**Tip:** Don't rely solely on the bookstore to bring in an audience. You'll need to market the event actively.

## Planning Your Book Reading Event

Here's a step-by-step plan to maximize attendance and make the most of your book reading:

1. **Send Out a Press Release:** Notify local media about your event.
2. **Get Featured in the Bookstore's Newsletter:** Ask if they can highlight your event in their email blast.
3. **Create a Promotional Postcard:** Offer to provide bag stuffers for the bookstore to hand out two weeks before the event.
4. **In-Store Signage:** Design an attractive poster that the bookstore can display to promote your reading.
5. **Point of Purchase Display:** If allowed, set up a small display featuring your book and information about the reading.

**Gratitude Tip:** Always send a thank-you note to the bookstore after the event. It's a simple gesture that can go a long way in building relationships.

## Tips for a Successful Book Reading

The structure of your book reading can make or break the event. Here's how to keep it engaging:

1. **Keep It Short and Sweet:** The ideal format is to read three excerpts, each lasting about **three to five minutes**.
2. **Encourage Q&A:** Leave at least **thirty minutes** for audience questions. Be prepared for a mix of questions about your book, writing process, and publishing experience.
3. **Bring Marketing Materials:** Have bookmarks, postcards, and business cards on hand to give away with each signed book.

4. **Develop a Catchphrase:** Create a signature message or catchphrase to include when you sign books.

5. **Capture the Moment:** Have a friend or professional take photos during the event. These can be shared on social media and added to your Amazon Author Central page.

**Recording Tip:** Record short video excerpts of your reading and post them on your YouTube channel, Facebook page, or website. It's a great way to extend the reach of your event.

# CHAPTER 12

## SUSTAINING MOMENTUM

While digital marketing is vital for promoting your book, there's nothing quite like the impact of **in-person appearances**. Whether it's a book reading, a speaking engagement, or attending a book festival, meeting potential readers face-to-face can help build a loyal fan base. Let's explore some effective strategies for leveraging these opportunities.

Book Readings: More Than Just Libraries

Book readings are a wonderful way to share your work directly with an audience, allowing you to connect on a personal level. While libraries are great venues, consider expanding beyond traditional spaces to attract a wider range of attendees.

1. Library Readings

Libraries love to support local authors, and many offer space for readings and discussions. Partner with the library staff for promotions, but don't solely rely on them. Here's how to make the most of it:

- **Promote Actively**: Invite your network, and encourage them to spread the word. Use social media, email newsletters, and local event listings.
- **Prepare an Engaging Presentation**: Instead of just reading an excerpt, include anecdotes, Q&A sessions, and stories about the writing process.

2. Unique Locations for Book Readings

Breaking out of the library mold can offer a unique experience. Hold your event at locations that resonate with the theme of your book:

- **For Adventure Books**: Try a mountaineering store.
- **For Romance Novels**: A cozy café or wine bar creates a perfect atmosphere.
- **For Gardening Books**: A local botanical garden or plant nursery offers a fitting backdrop.

The goal is to create an experience that aligns with your book's theme, making the event memorable and engaging for attendees.

## Speaking Engagements: Get Your Message Out

Public speaking is one of the most effective ways to promote your book and establish yourself as an expert. While it can seem daunting at first, it's a skill worth developing. Consider joining a **Toastmasters Club** to hone your public speaking abilities in a supportive environment.

## Local Opportunities for Speaking:

There are many local organizations and clubs that are often looking for speakers:

- **Rotary Clubs:** Great for community engagement.
- **Church Groups:** Many are open to hosting speakers, especially if your book aligns with their values.
- **Schools and Universities:** Ideal for books related to education, children's literature, or professional development.
- **Chambers of Commerce:** Business-focused audiences are perfect for nonfiction and self-help books.

**Pro Tip:** When selling books after your talk, bundle offers can be effective. For example:

- **Single Book:** $20
- **Bundle of Five:** $80 (a discount that incentivizes bulk buying)

## Participating in Book Festivals

Book festivals are vibrant events filled with avid readers, making them a great opportunity to showcase your work. However, they can be costly, so it's important to choose wisely.

## How to Choose the Right Festival:

1. **Research Entry Fees:** Some festivals charge significant fees, while others may offer free entry for authors. We recommend starting with local or regional festivals to minimize costs.
2. **Check for Speaking Slots:** Festivals often feature author panels or presentations. Apply early to secure a spot.
3. **Plan Your Display:** Use eye-catching materials like a retractable tabletop display. Sites like Post Up Stand offer

customizable, portable displays that make your table look professional.

## Collaborate with Other Authors

Networking with fellow authors can open doors to new promotional opportunities. Here are a few ways to collaborate:

- **Provide Testimonials**: Offer to write a blurb or testimonial for another author's book. This not only builds goodwill but also gets your name in front of their readers.
- **Write a Foreword**: If asked, writing a foreword for a fellow author's book can position you as an expert in your field.
- **Join an Anthology**: Participating in a genre-specific anthology can introduce you to a broader audience.

## Quick Tips for Selling Books at Events

When selling your book at in-person events, make it easy for people to make a purchase. A few simple tips:

- **Price It Right**: Stick to round numbers like $10, $15, or $20. This simplifies transactions, especially if you're handling cash.
- **Include Tax in the Price:** This avoids confusion and makes the process smoother.
- **Accept Multiple Payment Methods**: Bring a **Square Reader** or a PayPal card reader for credit card sales.

**Bonus Tip**: Bring plenty of change if you're handling cash sales. You don't want to lose a sale because you can't break a large bill.

## What to Bring to In-Person Events

Having the right materials can make a big difference in your sales and the overall experience for attendees. Here's a checklist:

1. **Books:** Bring more copies than you think you'll need.
2. **Marketing Materials:** Include bookmarks, postcards, and business cards.
3. **Display Signage:** A retractable banner or poster board of your book cover can make your table stand out.
4. **Order Forms:** Have forms on hand for customers who want to order later or prefer to purchase online.

### Selling Your Book in Gift Shops

**Gift stores, hospital shops, and cruise ship boutiques** can be fantastic venues for your book, especially if it fits a niche market. Consider your book's theme and identify relevant gift shops:

- **Hospital Gift Shops:** Ideal for self-help, inspirational, or health-related books.
- **Travel and Cruise Ship Stores:** Great for books related to travel, adventure, or escapism.
- **Coffee Shops and Cafés:** Perfect for fiction, poetry, and lifestyle books.

**Tip:** Approach the shop manager to ask how they source their products. Some work with distributors, while others buy directly from authors. Be prepared with a polished pitch about why your book is a good fit for their store.

### Partnering with Related Businesses

Books that align with specific industries can be sold directly through **related businesses.** If your book offers valuable content for professionals, companies may buy copies for events, employee gifts, or training purposes.

- **Leadership and Business Books:** Pitch your book to meeting planners or CEOs who might gift it to participants at conferences.

- **Lifestyle and Hobby Books:** For books about hobbies like hiking or gardening, approach relevant retail stores (e.g., outdoor gear shops or garden centers).
- **Children's Books:** Contact local toy stores, museums, or zoo gift shops, especially if the book's theme matches the venue.

This approach can help you sell bulk orders and build partnerships that lead to repeat sales.

## Selling at Unique Locations

Don't limit yourself to traditional venues. Hosting book readings or selling books at unique locations can open up entirely new audiences.

- **Specialty Stores:** If your book covers fitness or wellness, a gym or wellness center might be the perfect spot.
- **Themed Locations:** Choose locations that match your book's subject. For instance, if you've written about local history, a reading at a historical society or museum can attract interested readers.
- **Community Events:** Participate in farmers' markets, craft fairs, or local festivals. It's a great way to engage with your community and introduce your book to new readers.

## Fundraisers: A Win-Win Strategy

Partnering with local charities or organizations for a fundraiser is a fantastic way to promote your book while supporting a cause. Here's how it works:

- **Offer a Discounted Price:** Sell your book to the organization at a reduced cost, allowing them to sell it at retail price and keep the difference as a donation.

- **Bundle Sales**: Consider bundling your book with related products or offering signed copies for a higher donation value.

This approach helps spread the word about your book while giving back to the community, creating a positive image and good publicity.

## Book Cross-Promotion and Community Marketing

Engaging in cross-promotion with other authors or leveraging community resources can amplify your marketing efforts.

- **Joint Book Parties**: Team up with authors in your genre for a themed book party. It could be seasonal (e.g., a "Summer Reading Kick-Off") or based on a shared topic (e.g., travel or self-help).
- **Local Little Free Libraries**: Donate copies of your book to these neighborhood book exchanges. It's a great way to get your book circulating within the community.
- **Silent Auctions and Fundraisers**: Offer signed copies of your book as prizes for charity events. It's a fantastic way to gain exposure and support local causes.

**Bonus Idea:** Use BookCrossing.com to track your book as it travels from reader to reader around the world. It's a fun and interactive way to engage with your audience.

## eBook Promotions and Subscription Services

Services like **BookBub** and **Robin Reads** have gained popularity among self-published authors looking to promote their eBooks to dedicated readers. Here's how to make the most of these platforms:

1. **Heavily Discount Your eBook**: Most of these services recommend setting your eBook price to free or $0.99 for

the duration of the promotion. This strategy increases downloads and visibility, boosting your book's rankings.

- **Meet the Requirements**: Make sure your book has a professional cover, is well-edited, and has garnered several good reviews. These factors increase your chances of being accepted by premium services like BookBub.

- **Experiment with Different Services**: While BookBub is the gold standard, other services like **BookGorilla, The Fussy Librarian,** and **Freebooksy** offer similar models at a lower cost. Running promotions across multiple services can maximize your reach.

## Entering Book Contests

Participating in book contests can be an excellent marketing strategy. Winning or even being a finalist provides social proof and a sense of prestige. Here's how to get started:

- **Choose Reputable Contests**: Look for well-established contests that are known for their media coverage, such as the **Ben Franklin Awards** or the **IPPY Awards**.

- **Plan for Submission Fees**: Most contests require an entry fee, usually between $50 and $100, plus a few copies of your book. Budget accordingly.

- **Highlight Your Wins**: If you win or become a finalist, update your book cover with the award seal, add it to your Amazon description, and share the news on social media.

This recognition can significantly boost your book's visibility and credibility.

## Making It Easy to Buy

At every in-person event or appearance, make the purchasing process as seamless as possible:

- **Set a Round Price:** Avoid odd pricing like $18.99. Stick to $10, $15, or $20 for simplicity.
- **Offer Multiple Payment Methods:** Bring a Square or PayPal card reader to accept credit card payments, in addition to cash.
- **Include Bonuses:** Offer a small incentive for buying at the event, like a free bookmark or a signed copy.

The easier it is for people to buy, the more sales you'll make.

## Holiday Promotional Strategies

Timing your book promotions around holidays and special events can be a powerful way to boost sales. By aligning your book's theme with relevant holidays, you tap into the excitement and interest of the season. Here are some creative ideas to get started:

1. **Seasonal Specials:**
   - **Horror or Thriller:** Offer a special price or bundle deal for Halloween or Friday the Thirteenth.
   - **Romance:** Run a Valentine's Day promotion, emphasizing love-themed content.
   - **Self-Help and Wellness:** Launch a campaign in January for New Year's resolutions, offering a "Start Fresh" discount.
2. **Birthday Promotions:**
   - Celebrate your own birthday by offering your book at a special price. If you're turning forty, consider a 40 percent discount for that day only.
   - Use the year or era your book is set in for a themed promotion. For example, if your book is set in the 1980s, offer an "'80s Throwback" price.

3. Unique Holidays:
    - Utilize fun, lesser-known holidays for quirky promotions. Websites like Days of the Year offer a comprehensive list of unique holidays you can leverage (e.g., "National Coffee Day" for a book set in a coffee shop).

## Expanding Your Reach with Library Sales

The library market is often overlooked but can be a significant source of sales. With over **eighteen thousand public libraries** and **twenty-five thousand academic libraries** in the United States alone, tapping into this market is a must.

## Why Libraries?

Library readers are loyal and influential. When someone borrows your book from a library and loves it, they are likely to recommend it to others, boosting your sales indirectly. Libraries also provide exposure to readers who may not have purchased your book otherwise.

## Key Requirements for Library Sales:

1. **Quality Matters**: Your book must be professionally edited and well-designed. Libraries are discerning, and poorly made books are unlikely to make the cut.
2. **Cataloging in Publication (CIP) Data**: Having CIP data increases your chances of getting into libraries. It's not mandatory but offers credibility.
3. **Proper Binding**: Avoid spiral-bound books as they are less durable. Opt for paperback or hardcover editions.
4. **ISBN**: Ensure your book has an International Standard Book Number (ISBN), as it is essential for cataloging.

## Strategies for Selling to Libraries

1. **Submit to Library Trade Journals:**
   - The best way to get your book into libraries is through **library trade reviews**. Publications like **Library Journal, Booklist, Kirkus,** and **Publishers Weekly** are highly respected. If your book receives a positive review, it's likely to be purchased by multiple libraries.
   - Keep in mind that these reviews often need to be submitted **two to three months before publication**. Plan early to maximize your chances.

2. **Paid Review Services:**
   - If you don't manage to get a free review, consider using paid review services like **Kirkus Indie, Book Life Reviews,** or **Blue Ink Review**. While these services don't guarantee a positive review, they do guarantee a thorough and honest evaluation.
   - Paid reviews are also shared with library buyers, increasing your book's visibility among acquisition managers.

3. **Direct Outreach:**
   - Contact libraries individually, but remember that each one has its own purchasing process. Some libraries have centralized buyers for their district, while others purchase for individual branches.
   - Keep your pitch brief. Provide the ISBN and a short description of your book, and mention any awards it has won or if it has a local connection.

**Pro Tip:** Have friends and fans request your book at their local libraries. Patron requests can influence library purchase decisions significantly.

## Community Engagement and Joint Promotions

1. **Little Free Libraries:**
   - Donate copies of your book to Little Free Libraries in your area. It's a great way to get your book circulating locally and introduce it to new readers.
2. **Silent Auctions and Charity Events:**
   - Offering signed copies of your book as part of local fundraisers or silent auctions is a win-win. It raises funds for a good cause while providing exposure for your book.
3. **BookCrossing Program:**
   - Use BookCrossing.com to track your book's journey from reader to reader. It's an interactive way to engage with your audience and see where your book travels.

## Partnering with Businesses and Organizations

If your book aligns with a specific theme or industry, consider partnering with businesses or organizations that would benefit from bulk purchases.

1. **Corporate Sales:**
   - If your book offers insights on leadership or business strategies, pitch it to companies as a corporate gift. Meeting planners or HR departments might purchase copies for conferences or employee training sessions.
2. **Clubs and Associations:**
   - Approach clubs related to your book's theme. For instance, if your book is about fitness, connect with local gyms or running clubs. If it's about travel, contact travel clubs or RV associations.

3. **Museums and Specialty Shops:**
    - If your book's topic is historical or educational, museums and specialty shops (e.g., a mountaineering store for a hiking book) may be interested in stocking it.

### Joint Marketing Initiatives

Working with other authors can provide a boost to your marketing efforts:

1. **Co-Hosting Events:**
    - Collaborate with authors in your genre to host joint book signings or themed events. It's an effective way to reach each other's audiences.
2. **Cross-Promotion:**
    - Exchange email list features, promote each other's books on social media, or bundle books together for special promotions.

### eBook Promotion Platforms

Consider using services like **BookBub, BookGorilla,** and **The Fussy Librarian** to boost your eBook sales. These platforms connect your book directly with readers who have expressed interest in your genre.

### Tips for a Successful Campaign:

- Set a heavily discounted or free promotional price for a limited time.
- Ensure your book has a polished cover, solid reviews, and meets the platform's criteria.

1. Start a Meetup Group

Meetup groups are fantastic for building a community around your book's theme. They provide an opportunity for in-person and online discussions, making your book's content come alive for readers.

**Ideas for Meetup Groups:**

- **Social Media Guide:** If your book is about social media marketing, start a group for local entrepreneurs looking to learn social media tips.
- **Travel Enthusiasts:** If you've written a travel memoir, consider a monthly meetup with guest speakers sharing travel stories.
- **Business Development:** For a book on business or self-help, create a group focused on implementing strategies from your book.

**Pro Tip:** Promote your Meetup group across your social media platforms. Invite friends, colleagues, and readers to spread the word. This builds excitement and boosts attendance.

2. Create an Online Course

If your book is a nonfiction how-to or self-help guide, creating an online course can be a natural next step. An online course not only adds value to your readers but also establishes you as an authority on the topic. It's an excellent way to monetize your content while deepening your engagement with readers.

**Top Platforms for Hosting Courses:**

- **Skillshare:** A community-driven platform great for interactive courses.
- **Teachable and Thinkific:** Offer easy-to-use tools for building and marketing your course.

- **Udemy**: A well-known platform with a large audience, ideal for exposure.
- **Kajabi**: Best for creators looking to build a comprehensive digital business, including courses, email marketing, and more.

**Steps to Get Started:**

1. Outline your course content based on your book chapters.
2. Record video lessons and create supplementary materials (PDFs, quizzes).
3. Promote your course through your email list and social media channels.

3. **Amazon's KDP Select Program**

Amazon's **KDP Select** program can be an effective tool for boosting visibility and sales, especially during the initial launch phase. However, it does require a ninety-day period of exclusivity, so plan carefully.

**Key Features of KDP Select:**

- **Kindle Owner's Lending Library (KOLL)**: Your book is added to a library where Kindle owners can borrow it. You earn royalties based on the number of times your book is borrowed.
- **Free Book Promotions**: You can offer your book for free for up to five days during each ninety-day enrollment. This is a great way to attract new readers and get reviews.
- **Kindle Countdown Deals**: Run limited-time promotions with discounted pricing while still earning royalties. Readers love countdown deals for their urgency and perceived value.

**Bonus Perk**: Enrolling your book in KDP Select also makes it available on **Kindle Unlimited,** where you earn based on the number of pages read. This is particularly beneficial for fiction authors who often see higher engagement through Kindle Unlimited.

4. Keep the Momentum Going Beyond Two Years

The initial launch period may be over, but your book's life is far from done. Here are **eleven strategies** to maintain interest and boost sales even years after publication:

1. **Refresh Your Cover:** A new cover design can breathe life into an older book and attract new readers.
2. **Engage on Social Media:** Continue building your presence on your chosen platforms, sharing content related to your book's theme.
3. **Host Milestone Promotions:** Celebrate anniversaries of your book's release with special discounts or bonus chapters.
4. **Update Nonfiction Content:** For nonfiction, revise and update the information periodically. Release a new edition with fresh insights.
5. **Re-Release for Anniversaries:** Use significant anniversaries as an opportunity to relaunch your book with added content or a special edition.
6. **Promote Your Backlist:** If you publish a new book, include an excerpt of your first book in the back to drive interest.
7. **Kindle Singles:** For nonfiction, consider breaking out individual chapters as stand-alone **Kindle Singles** priced at $0.99 each.
8. **Leverage Speaking Engagements:** Offer discounted book bundles for event attendees.
9. **Create New Formats:** Expand your book into audio versions, children's editions, or workbooks.
10. **Develop a Workshop or Retreat:** Use your book's content to host a weekend retreat or online workshop, adding a new revenue stream.

11. **Launch a Webinar Series**: Turn your book's chapters into a series of webinars or mini-courses to reach a new audience.

### Community Involvement and Local Marketing

1. **Join Local Book Festivals**: Even years after your launch, book festivals offer a great platform for exposure. Engage with readers, network with other authors, and sell your book directly.
2. **Library Talks and Book Clubs**: Offer to give talks at local libraries or participate in book club discussions. Libraries often love featuring local authors, and book clubs provide intimate, engaged audiences.
3. **Little Free Libraries and BookCrossing**: Leave copies of your book in Little Free Libraries or use **BookCrossing.com** to track your book's journey from reader to reader. This grassroots approach helps create buzz.

### eBook Promotion Platforms

Consider tapping into eBook promotion services beyond the launch phase. Platforms like **BookBub, Freebooksy,** and **The Fussy Librarian** can boost your visibility by targeting readers who are already interested in your genre.

### Tips for Success:

- Heavily discount or offer your eBook for free during promotions to drive downloads.
- Ensure your book has a strong cover, a compelling blurb, and several positive reviews before submitting it to these platforms.

## Recap: A Lasting Impact

The journey of marketing your book doesn't end after the initial release phase. With the right ongoing strategies, you can extend the life of your book, reach new readers, and continue building your author brand.

**Remember:** Persistence and creativity are key. Explore different avenues, try new approaches, and don't be afraid to adapt your tactics based on what works best for your audience. Your book's success story is just beginning.

# CHAPTER 13

## BONUS: WRAP-UP CHAPTER: BRINGING IT ALL TOGETHER

As we conclude this journey through *Commonsense and Outcome-Driven Marketing for Authors*, I want to emphasize one final, critical point: The most successful authors don't just write books—they craft them with intention, clarity, and a deep understanding of their audience.

A great book doesn't start when you sit down to write—it begins long before, with a clear vision of who you are writing for and why.

At the very beginning of this book, we talked about the importance of defining your ideal reader—your book's avatar. This step is not just a recommendation; it's the foundation for everything that follows. If you skip this step or fail to refine it, you risk writing a book that lacks direction and, ultimately, an effective marketing plan.

Whether you are writing a family book, memoir, business growth book, passion project, authority-building nonfiction book, or a children's book, your ability to define, understand, and engage your audience will shape not only the book itself but also how you market and sell it.

But the work doesn't stop there.

📌 Pro Tip: 💡 If you can describe your ideal reader in detail before writing your book, you'll save time on rewrites, revisions, and ineffective marketing later. Define your avatar early!

**Revisiting Your Reader Avatar at Every Stage**

One of the most important lessons in this book is that marketing starts before the book is even written—but it doesn't end once the manuscript is complete. Let's break down the process into three critical stages:

1. Before You Write: Laying the Foundation

Think of this as the blueprint phase of your book. Just as a house needs a solid foundation before construction begins, your book needs a clear sense of purpose and audience.

Ask yourself:

Who is my ideal reader? (Be specific! "Women over forty" is too broad; "Busy working moms who want to start a side hustle" is better.)

What problem am I solving for them? (Even a family memoir solves a problem—helping future generations connect with their past.)

What will make my book different? (What unique perspective, experience, or expertise do you bring?)

📌 Pro Tip: 💡 If you're writing a nonfiction or authority-building book, make sure it aligns with your business, speaking goals, or consulting offers. A book is a tool—not just a product.

## 2. After the Book is Written (Before Marketing Begins): Refining Your Message

Many authors finish their manuscript and immediately start thinking about marketing—social media, Amazon ads, and book signings. But before you jump into tactics, pause. This is the time to refine your reader avatar once again and make sure everything aligns.

Does your book title and subtitle reflect the audience you originally envisioned?

Have you crafted a compelling book description that speaks directly to your reader?

Is your cover visually appealing to your specific audience? (A business book cover should not look like a children's book and vice versa.)

🔖 Pro Tip: 💡 Before locking in your title and subtitle, test different versions with potential readers. Use social media polls, email lists, or small focus groups to see which resonates most.

## 3. During Promotion & Sales: Targeted, Outcome-Driven Marketing

Marketing is not just about posting your book on social media and hoping for sales. It's about delivering the right message to the right people at the right time.

Here are key strategies based on your book type:

Family & Memoir Writers: Focus on storytelling and personal connections. Share anecdotes, family photos, and excerpts that create nostalgia. Target people who value legacy and preserving history.

Business & Growth-Focused Authors: Your book is a tool for positioning yourself as an expert. Use it to book speaking gigs, get media coverage, and establish authority in your field.

Children's Book Authors: Market to parents, teachers, and schools. Offer educational resources, coloring pages, or interactive storytelling sessions to engage your audience.

Self-Help or Educational Books: Highlight transformation. What will the reader gain? Show testimonials and case studies that reinforce your book's value.

Authority-Building Nonfiction Books: If your book is meant to establish credibility, leverage it for thought leadership. Use it as your "calling card" to land media appearances, podcast interviews, and speaking engagements.

Passion Project Books: These books are written from the heart, but they still need marketing. Focus on communities that share your passion—whether that's social media groups, niche forums, or events where your message resonates.

🔖 Pro Tip: 💡 Think beyond book sales! Your book can open doors to paid speaking engagements, online courses, consulting gigs, or business opportunities.

🔖 Pro Tip: 💡 Get testimonials from early readers. Whether it's an advanced review copy (ARC) team, beta readers, or clients, social proof sells books!

## Positioning Your Book for Podcasts, Speaking Engagements, and Media

For nonfiction and authority-building books, the real power comes from how you leverage the book beyond just selling copies.

🔖 Pro Tip: 💡 Create a one-sheet for podcast hosts and event planners. This should include your bio, key takeaways from your book, and why you'd be a great guest.

🔖 Pro Tip: 💡 When pitching yourself for podcasts or speaking gigs, don't just say, "I wrote a book." Lead with an interesting story, statistic, or challenge that ties into your book's topic.

🔖 Pro Tip: 💡 Want more PR? Sign up for **SourceBottle** and **PitchRate** because Reporters are looking for expert sources every day—you could be featured in an article, interview, or major publication!

## BONUS: WRAP-UP CHAPTER: BRINGING IT ALL TOGETHER

**Final Thoughts: Your Story Deserves to Be Shared**

Your book has the power to change lives—whether it's bringing families closer, teaching valuable lessons, helping people grow, or inspiring a child's imagination.

📌 Pro Tip: 💡 Your book's success isn't determined in the first week—it's a long game. Keep marketing consistently and repurpose your content across different platforms.

**Final Word**

Thank you for joining me on this journey. If you found this book helpful, I'd love to hear from you! Your feedback, success stories, and questions help me continue to provide valuable insights for authors like you.

📌 Pro Tip: 💡 Encourage reviews! Reviews help increase visibility on Amazon and other platforms. Politely ask readers to leave a review in your book's closing pages.

# CHAPTER 14

## BONUS: HOW TO AVOID A BAD PUBLISHING EXPERIENCE

As we come to the end of this book, it's crucial to address one of the most important aspects of your publishing journey—avoiding a bad experience. You've learned the ins and outs of book marketing and promotion, but none of that matters if your publishing process is full of headaches, unexpected costs, or subpar results.

This chapter serves as a cautionary guide to help you identify red flags, ask the right questions, and ensure that your publishing services provider meets your needs, ensuring a smooth, successful experience.

1. Step-by-Step Guidance

Ensure that your publishing services provider offers detailed, step-by-step guidance through every phase of the process—from production to distribution. A reputable publisher will walk you through important tasks like title brainstorming, cover design, production quality, and troubleshooting any issues that arise with services like Amazon or KDP.

Your provider should:

- **Guide you through every step**: Your provider should assist you from production to publication, including graphic feedback and quality control.

- **Create a vendor team**: Manage your vendors to stay on budget and within deadlines.

- **Troubleshoot common issues**: Whether it's problems with Amazon or KDP, your provider should handle the complexities that arise with third-party services.

- **Business Setup Assistance**: Help with setting up your book business, including acquiring a trade name, registering for sales tax, and organizing records.

- **Title Brainstorming and Pricing Research**: Collaborate with you to create an attention-grabbing title and determine the best price for your book through genre competition analysis.

- **Assist with Author Bio and Back-of-the-Book Blurb**: A good provider will work closely with you and the editor to draft these critical marketing pieces.

- **Provide Marketing and Launch Support**: From getting endorsements to coordinating an online book launch, they should support you in all facets of promotion.

If your provider isn't able to explain these steps or address your concerns, it's time to reconsider. Riley-Infinity Publishing offers comprehensive, tailored support, making sure every stage of your book's journey is handled professionally.

## BONUS: HOW TO AVOID A BAD PUBLISHING EXPERIENCE

2. **Vendor Team and Coordination**

Successful publishing requires a solid vendor team, including editors, designers, and marketing specialists. Make sure your publisher assembles the right team for your book and manages them effectively. They should serve as a liaison, handling communication and ensuring that timelines and budgets are respected. Ask if they provide quotes from each vendor so you know exactly what you're paying for.

3. **Budget Transparency and Fees**

One of the major issues authors face is unexpected fees. Before signing any agreement, make sure you have a clear understanding of all the costs involved, from the ISBN acquisition to layout design, cover art, and even re-upload fees for revisions. Will you be charged extra for formatting an eBook or hardcover edition? Is there a fee for each re-upload after revisions?

Always ask for an itemized breakdown of costs, and be cautious of vague pricing models. Here's what to look for:

- **Publishing Services Management Fee:** A flat fee for overseeing the entire project, from production to distribution.
- **Third-Party Services:** Includes developmental editing, line editing, proof-editing, cover design, and interior layout. These are typically invoiced by the vendors separately.
- **Revisions and Re-uploads:** Always clarify if there are extra charges for additional revisions or re-uploading files after making changes.

Here's an example of a cost breakdown for a manuscript:

- **Developmental Edit:** Paid half upfront and half upon completion.
- **Line Edit and Proof Edit:** Similar payment structure, paid in halves.

- **Cover Design:** Flat rate, including up to ten concepts and unlimited revisions.
- **Interior Layout:** Based on the complexity of layout elements.
- **eBook Conversion:** Initial estimates may change based on editing.
- **ISBN Costs:** Estimates for a ten-pack.
- **Miscellaneous Business Expenses:** May include sales tax licenses, domain registration, and trade name registration.

Ensure that all third-party services are transparently itemized, and ask for estimates upfront to avoid confusion. Any services outside the original scope may be billed at an additional hourly rate, so always confirm what's included in the initial estimate.

4. Customization and Personalization

Every book is different. Your publishing provider should customize their services to fit your book's unique needs. Whether it's selecting the right BISAC codes for genre categorization or helping you identify the best marketing tactics, a good publisher tailors their approach. A one-size-fits-all approach is a red flag.

5. Quality Control and Proofs

Reputable publishers will provide you with proofs before the final print, giving you a chance to review and make corrections. Always ensure that your service provider allows you to approve physical or digital proofs. This step is crucial for catching errors that could hurt the final quality of your book.

We at Riley-Infinity manage the proofing process and provide authors with one free revision upload to ensure your final product meets your standards.

## 6. Distribution and Royalties Management

Managing your book's distribution and royalties is a crucial aspect of the publishing process, and it's essential that your provider handles this efficiently. The logistics begin with setting up accounts on platforms like Amazon's KDP Print and Kindle for both print and eBook distribution. This includes everything from timing uploads, ordering proofs, and setting up national and international distribution to creating the "Look Inside the Book" feature on Amazon.

When it comes to royalties, transparency is key. You should be aware of how and when you will be paid, whether it's through direct deposits from Amazon or other retailers. Below is a general breakdown of royalties based on a typical nonfiction book priced at $16.95:

- **Direct Sales:** When you sell directly to consumers, your profit can be around $12.74 after deducting printing and shipping costs.
- **Amazon Sales:** If sold through Amazon, expect royalties of around $6.56.
- **Bookstore or Distribution Sales:** When sold through distribution partners or bookstores, royalties typically drop to about $3.17.
- **eBook Sales:** eBooks tend to offer higher royalties—around 70 percent. If priced at $6.99, you could expect roughly $4.89 per sale.

Make sure these details are clearly outlined in your contract, including the process for royalty payments and how any delays will be handled. Riley-Infinity ensures that all accounts are set up for direct deposits, allowing you to track your royalties and receive payments in a timely manner. Additionally, we provide guidance on ISBN acquisition, copyright legal pages, and revisions, ensuring every aspect of your book's distribution is taken care of.

Remember to confirm any fees for re-uploading files after revisions, as these may incur additional costs if the project changes significantly during production.

7. Post-Production Services

Post-production is often where many authors experience neglect. A good publisher will help optimize your Amazon Author Central page, ensure that your metadata is correctly filled out in Bowker (ISBN), and work to place your book in the best Amazon browse categories.

Riley-Infinity offers post-production support to optimize your book's visibility and make sure you're in the right categories for maximum discoverability.

8. Timeline Realism

An accurate timeline is essential for managing expectations and ensuring your project moves forward efficiently without sacrificing quality. Be cautious of publishers who promise rush jobs or quick turnarounds. While it's tempting to accelerate the process, doing so often leads to subpar results and unnecessary stress. A realistic timeline considers every phase of the project—from editing to final distribution.

Here's what a typical timeline might look like:

- **Developmental Edit:** ~One month (varies based on promptness of rewrites).
- **Copy Line & Proof Edit:** ~One month.
- **Proof Edit:** Three weeks.
- **Cover Design:** Ongoing during the editorial process.
- **Layout:** ~One month.
- **Printing:** One week for proofing, ~four weeks for physical inventory.

- **eBook Conversion:** One week (usually published a month after paperback).
- **Audiobook:** Two months (usually launched post-book release).

If your publishing provider rushes through these phases or offers to complete your project far quicker, it may result in missed steps and poor quality. Always ensure that the timeline is reasonable and allows room for revisions, cover design, layout, and production.

## 9. Client Responsibilities

A good publisher will make clear what's expected from you as the author. Whether it's providing materials, submitting an author bio, or approving cover designs, there are always tasks that you will need to complete. Make sure these responsibilities are communicated upfront to avoid delays.

Ensure that your provider clearly outlines your role in the process. What materials do you need to provide? Are there specific deadlines for submitting your bio, book blurb, or cover preferences? A lack of clarity here can lead to misunderstandings and delays.

We guide authors through every step and clearly define what we need from you to keep the project moving forward.

## 10. Confidentiality and Ownership

Make sure the company provides a confidentiality agreement and retains no ownership over your content. If they refuse, it's a red flag. Many providers outsource work overseas, leading to potential security issues and unexpected fees.

## 11. Best Effort and Termination Clauses

Ensure your provider has a best-effort clause and a clear termination policy. A reputable service should explain what happens at various stages (thirty, sixty, and 120 days) and clarify refund eligibility in case of cancellations.

## 12. Custom Services

Your provider should customize their services to your book's needs. Ask if they tailor their approach based on genre or specific goals, such as entering book awards or optimizing for Amazon categories. Riley-Infinity offers comprehensive solutions that adapt to each author's unique project.

## 13. Legal Considerations

Understand the legal implications of using song lyrics, quotes, or any copyrighted material in your manuscript. Your publisher should inform you of potential risks and guide you through the permission process, ensuring compliance with copyright law.

By asking these questions and ensuring transparency from the outset, you'll greatly reduce the chances of having a frustrating or costly publishing experience. At Riley-Infinity, we're committed to offering personalized, transparent, and secure services, ensuring you retain full ownership and control over your work. If you need assistance evaluating any proposals or have additional questions, we offer a free forty-five-minute consultation to help you make an informed decision.

## 14. Skipping Professional Editing

*Pitfall*: Authors sometimes skip proper editing, leading to unpolished manuscripts.
*How to Avoid*:

- **Invest in professional editing**: First, get a developmental edit to refine the structure, then a copyedit for grammar and style.
- **Hire vetted editors**: Use Reedsy, Fiverr, or Upwork, ensuring you review their credentials and request sample edits.

### 15. Ignoring Market Research

*Pitfall*: Some authors don't research their audience or market trends, leading to a poor fit for readers.
*How to Avoid*:

- **Research your genre**: Analyze bestsellers in your category on Amazon, Goodreads, and Kobo Writing Life.
- **Study trends**: Understand the themes, titles, and strategies successful authors in your genre use.

### 16. Neglecting Book Cover Design

*Pitfall*: A weak, generic cover design can cost you potential readers.
*How to Avoid*:

- **Hire an expert**: Book cover design is critical—work with a professional who specializes in book covers. Look on 99designs, Fiverr, or Reedsy.
- **Ensure it fits your genre**: Make sure the design resonates with your target audience and grabs attention.

### 17. Underestimating the Importance of a Marketing Plan

*Pitfall*: Launching without a marketing strategy leads to poor sales.
*How to Avoid*: Develop a comprehensive marketing plan that includes your target audience, goals, and promotional strategies like email campaigns, social media, and book events. Tools like **Mailchimp** (email marketing) and **Hootsuite** (social media management) can help streamline your efforts.

### 18. Not Building an Author Platform

*Pitfall*: Failing to engage with readers before and after the book launch weakens sales potential.

*How to Avoid*: Build an author platform early by establishing a social media presence, blogging, and maintaining a professional website. Platforms like **Instagram, Facebook,** and **X** allow you to connect with readers and share valuable insights.

### 19. Overlooking ISBN and Copyright

*Pitfall*: Skipping ISBN registration or neglecting copyright can lead to legal and distribution issues.

*How to Avoid*: Purchase an **ISBN** through Bowker and register your copyright with the U.S. Copyright Office. These steps ensure proper cataloging and protect your rights.

### 20. Setting Unrealistic Expectations

*Pitfall*: Authors often expect immediate success and high sales, leading to disappointment.

*How to Avoid*: Set achievable, researched goals. Understand that success takes time, and focus on long-term efforts such as regular content creation, networking, and staying updated on industry trends.

### 21. Neglecting Post-Publication Activities

*Pitfall*: Many assume the work is done after publishing, neglecting ongoing promotion.

*How to Avoid*: Continue marketing efforts through blog tours, social media, and book events. Gather reviews on platforms like **Amazon** and **Goodreads** to build credibility and keep your book relevant.

# CHAPTER 15

## BONUS: TOP TWENTY-FIVE PATHS TO SUCCESS FOR GOAL-DRIVEN AUTHORS

Success in the world of publishing doesn't just happen by chance—it's the result of careful planning, strategic actions, and knowing where to find the right tools and platforms to achieve your goals. Whether you want to sell a specific number of books, build your personal brand, or grow your platform, following these paths will help guide you.

### 1. Sell a Specific Number of Books

To sell a certain number of books, you'll need a solid marketing plan and the ability to leverage multiple platforms for distribution. Here's how to get started:

## Develop a Marketing Plan

A structured marketing plan is essential to achieving your sales goal. Start by defining your target audience, setting realistic timelines, and outlining promotional strategies such as social media campaigns, email marketing, and collaborations. These resources can help you refine your plan:

- **Mark Dawson's Self-Publishing Formula Podcast:** A great source for expert marketing advice tailored to self-published authors. You'll find tips on Amazon ads, email lists, and launching strategies.
- **Reedsy Blog:** Offers comprehensive guides, marketing resources, and strategies for authors. It's packed with free tools and advice to help you create a personalized marketing plan.
- **Amazon KDP University:** As the biggest platform for online book sales, learning how to navigate Amazon's marketing options (like ads, A+ content, and promotions) is crucial.

## Leverage Multiple Platforms

To maximize your book sales, diversify your distribution channels. Selling on multiple platforms increases your reach and ensures your book is accessible to different audiences.

- **Amazon KDP:** The leading platform for self-published authors, Amazon KDP provides extensive reach, visibility, and control over your book's pricing and marketing.
- **IngramSpark:** IngramSpark offers wider distribution than Amazon alone, reaching bookstores and libraries worldwide, making it essential if you want your book on shelves.
- **Barnes & Noble Press:** This platform gives you access to Barnes & Noble's established audience and offers both print and digital publishing options.

## 2. Build a Personal Brand

Building a personal brand is essential for long-term success as an author. Your brand should reflect your identity, your books, and the value you offer readers. Here's how to establish it:

**Develop a Professional Website**

Your website is the digital home of your author brand. It's where readers, media, and industry professionals will go to learn more about you and your work.

- **WordPress**: Known for its versatility, WordPress offers the highest level of customization. It's ideal if you want to add advanced features, blogs, or eCommerce to your site.
- **Squarespace**: User-friendly with beautiful templates, Squarespace makes it easy to design a professional-looking website without much technical knowledge.
- **Wix**: A great option for beginners, Wix offers simple drag-and-drop design functionality, making it affordable and easy to create a professional online presence.

Make sure your website includes key pages such as an "About" section, book pages, a blog, and a contact form. It should also be optimized for SEO to help readers find you easily through search engines.

**Build an Author Website**

Home Page

The home page is the first impression, so ensure it's clear, visually appealing, and highlights your author brand. Include:

- **Short Bio**: A concise, engaging introduction to who you are.

- **Professional Headshot**: Helps build credibility and connection.
- **Call to Action (CTA)**: Direct visitors to take action, like downloading your latest book.
- **Social Media Links**: Encourage interaction and follow-up on platforms like X or Instagram.

### About Page

The **About Page** is where you connect with readers on a deeper level by sharing your journey, inspiration, and writing background. Include:

- **Longer Bio**: Detail your writing journey and background, highlighting career achievements and personal elements that resonate with readers.
- **Call to Action**: Encourage readers to sign up for your newsletter or download a free resource.

### Books Page

This is the core of your site, showcasing your works in one place. Include:

- **Book Covers and Descriptions**: Showcase each book, providing enticing summaries and excerpts.
- **Purchase Links**: Offer easy access to platforms like Amazon, Kobo, and others for purchase.
- **Direct Purchase Option**: Consider allowing direct sales from your website for personalized signed copies.

### Use Your Website to Sell Books

Selling directly from your website is a powerful way to build your brand and increase profit margins. Here's how to optimize your website for sales:

### Payment Integration

Set up secure payment options using **PayPal, Square,** or **Stripe** to allow readers to purchase books directly from your site. Offering exclusive items like signed copies or limited editions adds value to these direct sales.

### Lead Magnets and CTAs

Use lead magnets like free chapters or exclusive content to capture email addresses and build your mailing list. Be sure to include clear CTAs throughout the site, inviting readers to buy your book, sign up for your newsletter, or download special offers.

### Landing Pages

Create specific landing pages for book launches or promotions. Each page should feature:

- A **clear CTA** (e.g., pre-order now or get your signed copy).
- A book summary, excerpt, and compelling imagery that reflects your genre.
- Links to reviews, endorsements, or testimonials from fans and influencers.

## Optimize SEO for Your Author Website

### On-Page SEO

Search Engine Optimization (SEO) is key to ensuring that readers and industry professionals can find your website. Focus on:

- **Keywords**: Incorporate relevant keywords, such as your book title, genre, and related terms, in headers, meta descriptions, and body text.
- **Image Alt Text**: Every image, especially your book cover, should have descriptive alt text for search engines.

- **Internal Linking:** Include links within your site to connect blog posts, book pages, and other important sections.

## Blogging for SEO

A regularly updated blog can improve your site's search engine ranking and drive more traffic. Write posts that provide value to your audience, such as writing tips, personal stories, or updates on your latest projects. By optimizing your blog for keywords, you improve your site's visibility and attract more visitors.

## Backlinks

Getting your site linked from reputable websites (e.g., book review sites, writing communities, or media outlets) boosts your SEO ranking. Be sure to submit guest posts to relevant blogs and participate in interviews or podcasts, linking back to your website.

## How to Sell Books Directly from Your Author Website

Selling books directly from your website allows for higher profit margins and personalized experiences for readers. Here's how to set it up effectively:

1. **Set Up E-Commerce Functionality**

Having a reliable e-commerce platform is key to managing book sales. Use plugins or integrations to make it easy for readers to purchase directly from your site.

- **Shopify:** Seamless integration with any website and great for selling digital and print books.
- **WooCommerce:** Ideal for WordPress users, it's highly customizable and supports physical and digital book sales.
- **Payhip:** Perfect for authors selling eBooks, audiobooks, or physical books. It's simple to use and has no upfront costs.

## 2. Set Up Digital Downloads

For authors selling eBooks or audiobooks, make sure to create a smooth digital download process.

- Use platforms like **Shopify** or **WooCommerce** to upload files and manage purchases.
- Ensure that readers can easily buy, download, and access your digital content. You may want to protect your content with DRM (Digital Rights Management) if desired.

**Top Three Tools for Digital Downloads:**

1. **Gumroad**: Best for selling eBooks directly and gathering customer emails.
2. **E-junkie**: A low-cost, reliable service for digital downloads and payments.
3. **BookFunnel**: Excellent for distributing eBooks securely and managing customer access.

## 3. Set Up Payment Processing

A reliable payment processor is essential for handling transactions. Ensure smooth payment options for your readers.

- **PayPal**: A trusted payment gateway for global users, integrating with most platforms.
- **Stripe**: Offers lower transaction fees and more customizability than PayPal.
- **Square**: Great for authors who attend in-person book signings and events, as it supports both online and physical transactions.

4. Offer Special Editions or Signed Copies

A huge benefit of selling directly is offering exclusive versions of your book.

- **Signed Copies:** Readers appreciate the personal touch of a signed physical book.
- **Special Bundles:** Combine formats (eBook + audiobook) or offer limited-edition cover art.
- **Exclusive Content:** Create unique editions with additional content like deleted scenes or author commentary.

5. Integrate Print-On-Demand (POD)

Instead of managing stock, print-on-demand services allow you to fulfill orders as they come.

- **Printful:** Integrates with Shopify and WooCommerce, handling printing and shipping.
- **Lulu:** Known for high-quality printing, Lulu works well for authors looking to offer professional-grade physical books.
- **Blurb:** Ideal for visually striking books, especially those with images or illustrations.

6. Offer Multiple Formats

Allow readers to choose between different formats like paperback, eBook, or audiobook.

- **ACX:** Distribute audiobooks on Amazon, Audible, and iTunes.
- **Draft2Digital:** A fantastic tool for distributing eBooks and paperbacks to a wide range of retailers.
- **Shopify:** Can be used to sell multiple formats (print, eBook, audiobook) directly from your site.

## 7. Promote Your Store

To drive traffic to your new bookstore, use various promotional strategies.

**Social Media:** Share exclusive offers, signed editions, or discounts with your followers.

**Email List:** Announce new books, sales, and limited-time offers to your subscriber list.

**Facebook & Google Ads:** Run targeted ad campaigns to direct readers to your store. You can also leverage **Amazon Ads** for specific book promotions.

By selling directly through your website, you not only keep more of the profits but also provide a personalized experience that readers love.

## Establish a Social Media Presence

Social media is a powerful tool for building and expanding your personal brand. It allows you to engage directly with readers, share updates, and build a community around your books.

- **Instagram:** With its visually-driven format, Instagram is perfect for authors who want to share behind-the-scenes content, book covers, quotes, and more. Use hashtags relevant to your genre to reach a broader audience.

- **Facebook:** Great for creating a more interactive space, Facebook allows you to build communities through groups, host live events, and have deeper conversations with your readers.

- **TikTok (BookTok):** TikTok is an ever-growing platform, and its "BookTok" community has become a hotspot for authors to promote their work. Short, engaging videos about your writing process, book recommendations, or character insights can attract a dedicated fan base.

## 3. Become a Bestseller

**Leverage Amazon Categories**

To become a bestseller, mastering the right **Amazon categories** is essential. You want to find categories with low competition but high demand to increase your chances of hitting the bestseller list. Use these tools to guide you:

- **Publisher Rocket**: Offers detailed insights into Amazon's book categories, helping you find the ones with low competition but strong potential.
- **BookBeam**: Provides comprehensive market insights, including trends and competitor analysis.
- **KDP Rocket by Dave Chesson**: A powerful tool for researching Amazon keywords and categories, ensuring your book reaches the right audience.

**Run a Pre-Order Campaign**

A well-planned **pre-order campaign** can drive excitement and build momentum before your book is even released. It also helps boost sales rankings on launch day.

- **Amazon KDP**: Allows authors to set up pre-orders for both Kindle and print books, making it easier to promote your book before its official release.
- **Gumroad**: A great platform to sell your book directly and build an email list simultaneously during the pre-order phase.
- **Smashwords**: Offers wide eBook distribution and makes it simple to set up a pre-order campaign across various retailers.

## 4. Generate Passive Income

**Set Up Automation**

Building a passive income stream requires smart automation. Setting up automated marketing and sales processes ensures you continue generating revenue without constant effort.

- **Kit:** This email marketing platform is perfect for setting up automated email sequences to promote your book and related content.
- **Hootsuite:** Automate and manage your social media posts, ensuring a consistent online presence without needing to post manually.
- **Mailchimp:** Known for its user-friendly interface, Mailchimp offers basic automation features for email marketing, allowing you to engage with readers regularly.

**Create Multiple Formats**

By offering your book in multiple formats—such as print, eBook, and audiobook—you can tap into different audience preferences and generate additional revenue streams.

- **ACX:** Transform your book into an audiobook, which is growing in popularity, especially for busy readers who prefer listening.
- **Lulu:** Provides a wide range of print-on-demand options, including hardbacks, so you can offer premium versions of your book.
- **Draft2Digital:** A fantastic platform for eBook and print distribution across wide retailers, giving your book more exposure.

## 5. Create a Legacy

### Preserve Ownership

Creating a legacy means ensuring you retain full control of your work. Platforms that prioritize ownership give you the flexibility to manage your book's pricing, royalties, and rights.

- **Amazon KDP:** Provides complete control over royalties and pricing while allowing authors to maintain ownership of their work.
- **IngramSpark:** A trusted platform for self-publishing with flexible terms on ownership, offering wide distribution.
- **Riley-Infinity:** Offers personalized support, ensuring authors keep full rights and control over their intellectual property.

### Consider Archiving

Archiving your book ensures that it is preserved for future generations, creating a long-lasting impact.

- **Library of Congress:** Archiving your book here guarantees that it will be stored for historical purposes and available for future generations.
- **Goodreads:** Allows readers to discover and discuss your book, creating a lasting record of your work.
- **National Archives:** Ideal for personal stories or family histories, preserving your book for posterity.

## 6. Establish Credibility in a Field

### Write Authoritatively

Establishing credibility as an author requires producing high-quality, well-researched content. By drawing from authoritative sources, you can add depth and legitimacy to your writing. Use these top sources for research and data:

- **Google Scholar**: Access thousands of peer-reviewed articles, research papers, and studies across multiple disciplines.
- **JSTOR**: A vast digital library of academic journals and scholarly articles for deep research.
- **PubMed**: Ideal for authors writing in scientific or medical fields, providing access to research papers and clinical studies.

**Network with Industry Experts**

Connecting with leaders in your field is key to building credibility and staying informed. These platforms make networking easier:

- **LinkedIn**: The most widely used platform for professional networking. Create meaningful connections and join industry-relevant groups.
- **Clubhouse**: Participate in live audio discussions with experts and thought leaders, contributing to important conversations in your niche.
- **X**: Follow and engage with industry influencers, contributing to trending discussions while expanding your network.

## 7. Drive Leads to a Business

**Include a CTA in Your Book**

If your goal is to drive leads to your business, including an effective **Call to Action (CTA)** in your book is essential. Whether it's inviting readers to visit your website, subscribe to a newsletter, or schedule a consultation, an engaging CTA can convert readers into leads.

- **Canva:** Design visually appealing CTAs to place throughout your book and marketing materials.
- **Leadpages:** Create compelling landing pages with CTAs that drive readers to take action.
- **OptinMonster:** Build custom popups and lead capture forms to engage readers at key moments.

### Offer a Lead Magnet

A **Lead Magnet** is a valuable free offer, such as an eBook or checklist, that encourages readers to share their email addresses in return. This strategy helps build your email list while driving business leads.

- **Kit:** A powerful tool for creating email forms and automating the delivery of lead magnets to new subscribers.
- **Mailchimp:** Offers features for collecting emails and auto-delivering lead magnets through campaigns.
- **Sumo:** Great for lead generation, Sumo allows you to create on-site forms and popups that promote your lead magnet.

## 8. Build an Email List

### Include a Sign-up Link

Building an email list is one of the most effective ways to maintain long-term engagement with your audience. Including a clear and compelling sign-up link on your website, in your book, or through social media can help you gather email subscribers.

- **Mailchimp:** With a free-tier option, Mailchimp is a popular tool for email list building and managing campaigns.
- **Kit:** Specially designed for creators and authors, Kit makes it easy to grow and engage with your list.

- **MailerLite:** A user-friendly option offering free features to help you create and grow your email list.

### Collaborate with Other Authors

Collaborating with other authors is a great way to expand your reach and build your email list by tapping into their audiences.

- **StoryOrigin:** A platform that helps authors collaborate on promotions, email list building, and reader swaps.
- **BookFunnel:** Use this tool to organize group promotions and gather emails from new readers.
- **Prolific Works:** Create book giveaways to expand your email list while boosting visibility within your genre.

## 9. Launch a Career as an Author

### Join Writing Groups

One of the best ways to develop as a writer and build a career is by joining writing communities. These groups provide valuable feedback, networking opportunities, and support from fellow authors. Here are three highly recommended writing communities:

- **Scribophile:** Known for serious critiques from fellow writers, this community helps improve your work through detailed feedback.
- **Writers' Café (on Kboards):** A space where experienced authors offer advice, tips, and encouragement.
- **Critique Circle:** A long-standing group for writers to receive constructive feedback on their drafts.

### Enter Competitions

Competitions can offer validation, exposure, and prizes that help launch your writing career. Many authors gain their first break through writing contests. The top three competitions are:

**Writer's Digest Annual Competition:** Open to writers of all genres, offering exposure and monetary rewards.

**The Bridport Prize:** An international competition that offers prestige and recognition to winners across genres.

**The Bath Novel Award:** Aimed at unpublished and self-published authors, this competition offers a significant platform to launch careers.

## 10. Create a Series of Books

### Plan Ahead

Creating a book series requires careful planning and continuity between books. To maintain a consistent storyline and character development, you'll need effective planning tools:

- **Scrivener:** A favorite writing software for authors planning multiple books, Scrivener helps organize notes, research, and storylines.
- **Plottr:** A visual tool that allows you to map out plotlines, character arcs, and settings across multiple books.
- **Trello:** A flexible project management tool that can help you organize ideas, timelines, and character development for your series.

### Market Consistently

Marketing a series involves engaging readers continuously. You can run ads for each new release or promote the entire series at once. Here are the top marketing tools for book series:

- **BookBub Ads:** An excellent platform for targeted ads to readers of your genre, offering great reach to the right audience.
- **Facebook Ads:** Use Facebook's audience-targeting features to create lookalike audiences based on your existing readers.

- **Amazon Ads:** Run campaigns for individual books or the entire series, leveraging Amazon's platform to drive sales.

## 11. Get Media Coverage

### Craft a Strong Press Kit

A professional press kit is essential when seeking media coverage for your book. It includes your bio, book synopsis, reviews, and other relevant information to make it easy for journalists to cover your story. Here are the top tools to create a press kit:

- **Canva:** Use Canva's templates to design a polished press kit that includes visuals and essential details.
- **Fiverr:** Hire freelancers to create a professional press kit, ensuring it meets media standards.
- **Venngage:** A graphic design tool that helps you build engaging visual press kits to stand out from the crowd.

### Reach Out to Local Media

Local media can offer a powerful platform to raise awareness about your book. Connect with journalists using these platforms:

- **Muck Rack:** A tool to find journalists and writers in your niche who may be interested in covering your book.
- **SourceBottle:** A free online platform that connects journalists, bloggers, and content creators with expert sources. It offers opportunities for giveaways and case studies, making it versatile for various media needs.
- **Pressfarm:** A PR tool that helps authors get in touch with relevant journalists and media outlets to promote their work.

## 12. Build a Large Email Subscriber List

### Create a Lead Magnet

One of the most effective ways to grow your email list is by offering a **lead magnet**—a free, valuable resource in exchange for a reader's email address. Popular options include a free book sample, exclusive behind-the-scenes content, or access to a special Q&A session.

- **Free Book Sample:** Offer the first chapter of your book to entice readers.
- **Exclusive Content:** Share never-before-seen material, like character backstories or extended scenes.
- **Q&A Session:** Provide access to a private session where readers can ask questions about your writing process or characters.

### Add Subscription Forms on Website

Make sure your website prominently features email sign-up forms. Use **Mailchimp** or **Kit** to manage these forms, setting up popups, sidebars, and dedicated landing pages to capture leads. Placing subscription forms on multiple parts of your website increases the chances of readers signing up.

### Promote on Social Media

Share your lead magnet on social media platforms like Facebook, X, and Instagram to drive traffic to your sign-up forms. Use **targeted ads** on platforms like Facebook and Instagram to offer free downloads in exchange for email sign-ups, reaching audiences that are more likely to engage with your content.

### Collaborate with Other Authors

Join forces with other authors in your genre to cross-promote newsletters or lead magnets. Platforms like **StoryOrigin**,

**BookFunnel,** and **Prolific Works** allow authors to collaborate on giveaways and promotions that help expand your email list by sharing audiences.

**Top Three Tools to Build and Manage Email Lists:**

1. **Kit:** Tailored for authors, offering advanced automation.
2. **Mailchimp:** A user-friendly email marketing tool with free options.
3. **MailerLite:** Offers built-in landing pages and free-tier features.

## 13. Create a Loyal Fanbase

**Consistent Engagement**

To create a loyal fanbase, you need to communicate regularly with your readers through newsletters, blog posts, and social media. Share personal insights about your writing journey and respond to comments to build a deeper connection. Regular updates keep your audience engaged and invested in your success.

**Exclusive Content**

Offering perks to your most loyal readers can create a sense of community. Consider creating special content like early access to book drafts, exclusive stories, or a behind-the-scenes look at your writing process. Platforms like **Patreon** or private Facebook groups are ideal for delivering this content to superfans.

**Offer Signed Copies or Limited Editions**

Nothing creates loyalty like offering something special to your fans. Using services like **Blurb** or **Lulu,** you can produce signed or limited-edition copies of your book for your most dedicated readers, adding value that goes beyond the regular book format.

### Run Contests and Giveaways

Organize contests or giveaways to keep your readers excited and engaged. Offer prizes like signed copies, exclusive swag, or early access to new content. Use tools like **Rafflecopter** or **Gleam** to run these contests seamlessly across your website and social media.

### Top Three Platforms for Fan Engagement:

1. **Patreon:** Offer exclusive content and perks to paying superfans.
2. **Facebook Groups:** Create private spaces for discussions and exclusive content.
3. **Discord:** Build a real-time community where fans can interact with you directly.

## 14. Successfully Launch Your First Book

### Plan the Launch

A successful book launch begins with careful planning. Set up a timeline at least three to six months in advance, outlining tasks like cover reveals, social media promotion, and ARC distribution. During this prelaunch phase, focus on building excitement and momentum leading up to the release date.

### Create a Pre-Order Campaign

Pre-orders not only boost sales but also improve your chances of ranking higher on platforms like Amazon. Offer incentives such as discounts, signed copies, or bonus content to encourage readers to pre-order. Set up pre-orders on **Amazon, Kobo,** and your own website using platforms like **Shopify** or **Blurb.**

### Engage Influencers and Bloggers

Reach out to book bloggers and influencers in your genre to gain reviews and mentions ahead of your book's release. Platforms like **NetGalley** and **BookSirens** allow you to distribute ARCs to key reviewers who can generate early buzz for your book.

### Host a Virtual Book Launch

Virtual book launches offer a great way to engage with fans and celebrate the release of your book. Use platforms like Facebook, Instagram, or YouTube to host a live event where you can read excerpts, offer giveaways, and share behind-the-scenes stories. Engage with your audience in real time to create a memorable experience.

### Top Three Resources to Organize a Book Launch:

1. **BookFunnel:** Ideal for distributing ARCs and growing your email list.
2. **NetGalley:** A trusted platform for securing early reviews from librarians, bloggers, and media.
3. **Rafflecopter:** Perfect for running giveaways to generate excitement and build momentum before launch day.

## 15. Win Awards and Recognition

### Research Awards

Winning awards can significantly boost your credibility and increase visibility. Research awards that are relevant to your genre and publication status, such as the **IPPY Awards, Reader's Favorite Awards,** and **Indie Book Awards.** These provide great opportunities for recognition in the independent publishing community.

### Follow Submission Guidelines

Each award has its own criteria, including book length, publication date, and entry fees. Keep a calendar of deadlines and ensure you provide all required materials.

### Promote Wins and Nominations

Once your book wins or is nominated, add award badges to your book cover, website, and social media profiles. Announce the achievement in your newsletter and send out press releases to gain further attention.

### Top Three Places to Find and Submit to Awards:

1. **Writer's Digest:** Lists various reputable literary contests.
2. **ALLi (Alliance of Independent Authors):** Offers curated lists of awards for indie authors.
3. **BookLife Prize:** A well-regarded indie book award program run by Publishers Weekly.

## 16. Land Bookstore Distribution

### Optimize Your Book's Presentation

Before approaching bookstores, ensure your book looks professional. This includes high-quality cover design, formatting, and editing. Use POD services like **Blurb** or **Lulu** to print high-quality copies that meet bookstore standards.

### Approach Local Bookstores

Start with smaller, independent bookstores, offering to consign your book or host a book signing event. Attend local events and build relationships with store managers for more opportunities.

### Use Distribution Services

Distributors like **IngramSpark** and **Baker & Taylor** are key to getting your book listed in catalogs that bookstores use to order inventory. Ensure your book has an ISBN and is available through these major distributors.

Top Three Resources for Distribution:

1. **IngramSpark:** Comprehensive distribution to bookstores and libraries.
2. **Blurb:** Integrated POD and bookstore distribution services.
3. **Bookshop.org:** Sell through local indie bookstores online.

## 17. Turn Your Book into a Movie/TV Show

### Create a Compelling Script or Treatment

To pitch your book as a film or TV show, you'll need a well-developed screenplay or treatment. If needed, hire a professional screenwriter to adapt your story for the screen.

### Pitch to Producers or Agents

Research and approach producers, production companies, or literary agents that specialize in book-to-film adaptations. Platforms like **Stage 32** and **InkTip** are great for connecting with industry professionals.

### Enter Adaptation Competitions

Competitions can offer your book exposure to industry insiders, increasing your chances of an adaptation.

### Leverage Social Media Buzz

Use social media platforms like X or TikTok to show producers that your book has a built-in audience. Fan engagement and social buzz can demonstrate the potential for a successful adaptation.

Top Two Resources for Film/TV Adaptation:

1. **InkTip**: Connect with producers and agents to pitch your book.

2. **Stage 32**: An industry networking platform connecting authors with filmmakers and screenwriters.

# CHAPTER 16

## TOOLS AND TEMPLATES FOR AUTHORS

Creating a successful book requires more than just writing. You'll need the right tools to help streamline your process and enhance the quality of your work. Here are some essential tools for writing, editing, and proofreading.

1. Writing and Organization Tools

**Scrivener**

*Description*: Scrivener is a powerful writing software tailored for authors. It's designed to help you organize your manuscript, research, and notes in one place, making it easy to manage large writing projects, whether fiction or nonfiction.

*Key Features*:

- **Corkboard:** Helps visualize scenes with index cards.
- **Document Management:** Organizes chapters, research, and notes within the project.
- **Compilation:** Export your manuscript into different formats (e.g., ePub, PDF).

*Why Use It*: Scrivener is ideal for authors who prefer a structured approach to writing, allowing you to break your project into manageable pieces. It also simplifies the process of exporting your work in professional formats for publishing.

## Google Docs

*Description*: Google Docs is a free, web-based word processor that offers real-time collaborative writing and editing. It's an excellent choice for authors working with beta readers, co-authors, or editors who need to collaborate remotely.

*Key Features*:

- **Collaboration:** Share documents and get real-time feedback.
- **Comments and Suggestions:** Collaborators can leave comments or suggest edits.
- **Accessibility:** Access from any device with an internet connection.

*Why Use It*: Google Docs is perfect for authors who need to collaborate frequently or work on-the-go. Its intuitive design and collaboration features make it one of the easiest tools for managing writing projects and feedback.

2. Editing and Proofreading Tools

**Grammarly**

*Description*: Grammarly is an AI-powered tool that checks your grammar, punctuation, and writing style, helping improve the overall quality of your manuscript. It can detect errors in real time and suggest improvements to your sentence structure, tone, and vocabulary.

*Key Features*:

- **Real-Time Feedback**: Instantly identifies grammar, punctuation, and style mistakes.
- **Plagiarism Checker**: Ensures your work is original (available with the premium version).
- **Browser Extension**: Works across different platforms like email, social media, and word processors.

  *Why Use It*: Grammarly helps authors polish their drafts quickly and easily, ensuring your book is grammatically sound before sending it to an editor.

**ProWritingAid**

*Description*: ProWritingAid is a comprehensive editing tool that goes beyond grammar and spelling checks. It offers detailed reports on readability, structure, pacing, and style, making it a go-to tool for authors who want a deeper analysis of their work.

*Key Features*:

- **In-Depth Reports**: Provides feedback on structure, clarity, readability, and writing style.
- **Integration**: Works with platforms like Scrivener, Google Docs, and MS Word.
- **Customizable Reports**: Tailor feedback to your specific goals as a writer.

*Why Use It*: ProWritingAid is perfect for authors looking for a more detailed and analytical approach to editing, providing deeper insights into writing structure, flow, and readability.

3. Self-Publishing Platforms

**Amazon Kindle Direct Publishing (KDP)**

*Description*: KDP is a leading platform for self-publishing, enabling authors to publish eBooks and paperbacks directly on Amazon. *Key Features*:

- **User-Friendly Interface**: Uploading manuscripts and covers is streamlined.
- **Royalties**: Earn up to 70 percent on eBook sales.
- **Global Reach**: Your book becomes available to millions of readers worldwide. *Why Use It*: KDP offers easy access to Amazon's vast marketplace, making it a popular choice for authors aiming for wide exposure and profitability.

**IngramSpark**

*Description*: A comprehensive self-publishing platform that specializes in print-on-demand and extensive distribution options. *Key Features*:

- **Wide Distribution**: Reaches bookstores, libraries, and online retailers.
- **Professional Printing**: High-quality hardcover and paperback printing.
- **User-Friendly Dashboard**: Simplifies managing your books and tracking sales. *Why Use It*: IngramSpark excels in providing wide distribution and professional print options, making it ideal for authors seeking both digital and physical presence in bookstores and libraries.

## Templates for Authors

### Book Outline Template

*Purpose*: This template helps authors structure their manuscripts, organize chapters, and outline key plot points for a smooth writing process. *Contents*:

- **Book Title:** Placeholder for your title.
- **Genre:** Specify your book's genre.
- **Target Audience:** Identify your intended readers.
- **Chapter Breakdown:** Space for chapter titles, summaries, and key events.
- **Character Profiles:** Sections for character names, traits, and arcs.
- **Themes and Motifs:** Highlight recurring themes or ideas.

*Example Template*:

- **Book Title:** Insert Title Here
- **Genre:** Insert Genre Here
- **Target Audience:** Insert Audience Here

**Chapter Outline:**

- **Chapter 1**: Title
    - Summary: Brief Description
    - **Key Events:** List Key Events
- **Chapter 2**: Title
    - Summary: Brief Description
    - **Key Events:** List Key Events

Character Profiles:

- **Character Name:** Insert Name
  - Traits: Insert Traits
  - Arc: Insert Character Arc

*Why Use It*: A well-organized book outline serves as a roadmap for your writing, helping you stay focused, structure your story, and ensure cohesive character development.

## Marketing Plan Template

### Purpose

A marketing plan is essential for any author aiming to promote their book effectively. It provides a roadmap for reaching target readers, achieving sales goals, and maximizing visibility.

### Contents

- **Book Title and Description:** Clearly define your book and its key selling points.
- **Target Audience:** Identify who your ideal readers are.
- **Marketing Goals:** Set clear objectives such as increasing sales or growing a mailing list.
- **Marketing Strategies:** Define tactics like social media campaigns, book tours, or influencer outreach.
- **Timeline:** Schedule key milestones and promotional activities.
- **Budget Overview:** Include estimates for ads, promotional materials, or book events.

### Example Template

**Book Title:** Insert Title Here
**Description:** Brief overview of the book's content and appeal

**Target Audience:** Insert Audience Here

**Marketing Goals:**

1. Goal 1: e.g., Sell five hundred copies in the first month
2. Goal 2: e.g., Grow email list by one thousand subscribers
3. Goal 3: e.g., Secure media coverage from five outlets

**Marketing Strategies:**

- Strategy 1: Launch Instagram ad campaign targeting readers of similar genres
- Strategy 2: Organize virtual book tour with bloggers and influencers
- Strategy 3: Engage readers through weekly newsletter updates

**Timeline:**

- **Date:** Book cover reveal on social media
- **Date:** Launch giveaway on Facebook and Instagram
- **Date:** Start sending out Advanced Reader Copies (ARCs)

**Budget Overview:**

Social media ads: $500
Virtual tour expenses: $200
ARC copies and shipping: $150

**Why It's Important**

A well-structured marketing plan helps you focus your efforts, allocate resources wisely, and measure progress, ensuring your book gets the attention it deserves. This template acts as a guide to define your goals and execute them with clarity and efficiency.

## Author Website Checklist

**Purpose:**

To ensure authors build an effective website with all key components for audience engagement, book sales, and a professional online presence.

**Contents:**

1. **Domain Name and Hosting:**
   - Secure a memorable domain (e.g., yourname.com) with reliable hosting through providers like Bluehost or SiteGround.
2. **Professional Design:**
   - Opt for a clean, responsive layout that works on all devices, focusing on ease of navigation and a design that reflects your brand.
3. **About the Author Page:**
   - Include a detailed bio highlighting your background, writing journey, and accomplishments. Add a professional headshot to personalize the page and help readers connect with you.
4. **Books Page:**
   - Create a page showcasing your published works, including cover images, blurbs, and links to purchase. Each book should have its own section with detailed descriptions and purchase options (Amazon, direct sales, etc.).
5. **Blog/News Section:**
   - Keep readers engaged with regular blog posts or updates about your writing journey, insights, upcoming events, and book-related content. A blog also helps boost your SEO, increasing website visibility.

6. **Contact Page:**
    - Provide an easy way for readers, media, and collaborators to get in touch via a simple contact form or a dedicated email address.
7. **Newsletter Sign-Up Form:**
    - Integrate an email sign-up form on your site to grow your mailing list, offering incentives like a free chapter or bonus content to encourage sign-ups.
8. **Social Media Links:**
    - Include icons linking to your social media profiles (e.g., X, Instagram, Facebook) so readers can follow and engage with you across platforms.
9. **Privacy Policy and Terms of Use:**
    - Ensure your website includes legal pages such as a Privacy Policy and Terms of Use to comply with regulations and protect user data. These are especially important if you are collecting email addresses or selling directly from your site.

**Example Checklist:**

**Author Website Checklist:**

- ☐ Domain Name and Hosting
- ☐ Professional Design
- ☐ About the Author Page
- ☐ Books Page
- ☐ Blog/News Section
- ☐ Contact Page
- ☐ Newsletter Sign-Up Form
- ☐ Social Media Links
- ☐ Privacy Policy and Terms of Use

## Step-by-Step Timelines for Different Goals Checklist

Creating specific timelines for different author goals ensures a clear path to success. Below is an example of how to break down tasks over a set period to achieve key objectives.

Example Timelines:

1. **Goal: Build an Email List in Six Months**

   - **Month 1:** Create a lead magnet (e.g., free chapter, exclusive content) to entice sign-ups.
   - **Month 2:** Set up email capture forms and automation on your author website using tools like Mailchimp or Kit.
   - **Month 3:** Promote your lead magnet on social media (Instagram, Facebook, X) and engage readers with valuable content.
   - **Month 4:** Nurture relationships by sending exclusive content to your subscribers, such as behind-the-scenes looks at your writing process or special offers.
   - **Month 5:** Run a giveaway for signed books or merchandise to attract new subscribers.
   - **Month 6:** Review and optimize your email marketing strategy by analyzing open rates, click-throughs, and subscriber feedback. Adjust messaging or frequency if needed.

2. **Goal: Launch Your First Book in One Year**

   - **Months 1–3:** Start with foundational tasks like finalizing your manuscript, hiring an editor, and choosing a book cover designer.
   - **Months 4–6:** Build your author website, and develop a prelaunch marketing plan. Create social media accounts and start posting about your book journey.

- **Months 7–9:** Finalize the book layout, work on the interior design, and set up distribution channels like Amazon KDP or IngramSpark. Begin gathering early reviews.
- **Months 10–12:** Launch the book! Host a virtual or in-person book launch event, run pre-order campaigns, and leverage influencer or blogger outreach. Promote the book consistently through social media and email newsletters.

3. **Goal: Expand Your Fanbase in Nine Months**

- **Month 1:** Establish or revamp your social media profiles (Instagram, Facebook, X, Goodreads) to align with your author brand.
- **Month 2:** Begin engaging with your audience by posting regularly, asking for feedback, and running polls or Q&A sessions.
- **Months 3–4:** Create exclusive content (e.g., bonus chapters or behind-the-scenes videos) and offer it as a freebie for email sign-ups.
- **Months 5–6:** Host contests, giveaways, or live events to deepen engagement with current fans and reach new ones.
- **Months 7–9:** Collaborate with other authors or influencers in your niche. Join author groups, and cross-promote your work to widen your reach.

4. **Goal: Create an Author Website in Three Months**

- **Month 1:** Register your domain name and choose a website platform (WordPress, Squarespace, Wix). Plan out key content, such as your About page, Books page, and Contact form.

- **Month 2:** Design your website and begin creating essential pages. Optimize the site for SEO and set up a blog or news section.
- **Month 3:** Test all functionality (forms, links, e-commerce) and launch your site. Begin promoting it on social media and through email.

5. **Goal: Grow Your Instagram Audience in Six Months**

- **Month 1:** Audit your current Instagram account or create a new one with a clear bio, professional profile image, and brand-aligned visuals.
- **Month 2:** Develop a posting strategy using themes such as writing tips, book quotes, personal insights, and behind-the-scenes content.
- **Month 3:** Begin using targeted hashtags and engaging with relevant accounts (authors, readers, book clubs) to increase visibility.
- **Month 4:** Launch a content series (e.g., weekly writing prompts or character features) to encourage consistent engagement.
- **Month 5:** Collaborate with other creators through take-overs, shout-outs, or reels to expand reach.
- **Month 6:** Analyze performance data and adjust your content schedule and tone accordingly to maintain steady growth.

6. **Goal: Pitch to Podcasts and Media Outlets in One Year**

- **Months 1–2:** Research relevant podcasts, blogs, and digital media outlets that align with your genre, audience, or author journey.
- **Months 3–4:** Create a professional media kit, including your author bio, book synopsis, high-res images, and interview topics.

- **Months 5–6:** Begin pitching to podcasts and media outlets. Personalize each pitch and highlight why your story is a good fit.
- **Months 7–8:** Follow up on unanswered pitches and continue reaching out to new platforms. Track all communication in a spreadsheet.
- **Months 9–10:** As interviews are booked, promote appearances across your website, email list, and social channels.
- **Months 11–12:** Compile and repurpose media content (clips, quotes, testimonials) into promotional materials for future outreach.

7. **Goal: Create and Launch an Online Course in Nine Months**

   - **Months 1–2:** Identify your course topic and audience. Map out key lessons, outcomes, and delivery format (video, audio, PDF).
   - **Months 3–4:** Develop course materials and record content. Choose a platform such as Teachable, Thinkific, or Kajabi or a fully integrated website where you can also host your course content.
   - **Month 5:** Begin building your course landing page and email sequence for your waitlist.
   - **Month 6:** Invite beta users for feedback and testimonials. Make final refinements to your course.
   - **Months 7–8:** Open enrollment with a promotional launch campaign using email, social media, and partnerships.
   - **Month 9:** Monitor course performance, engage with students, and plan for future evergreen or live relaunches.

8. **Goal: Get 25 Book Reviews in Six Months**

   - **Month 1:** Build a list of potential reviewers, including ARC readers, bloggers, and supportive fans.

- **Month 2:** Distribute free advance copies in exchange for honest reviews on Amazon, Goodreads, and other relevant platforms.
- **Month 3:** Follow up with gentle reminders and thank reviewers who post.
- **Month 4:** Create a social media post or graphic encouraging more readers to leave reviews.
- **Month 5:** Run a small giveaway or contest where reviews serve as entries.
- **Month 6:** Celebrate reaching your review milestone publicly and feature top reviews in your marketing.

And on, and on, there are so many amazing things you can do with your book and we can help with them all if you need us.

# APPENDIX

## ADDITIONAL TOOLS AND RESOURCES FOR SELF-PUBLISHED AUTHORS

This appendix provides a list of essential tools, platforms, and services that can aid self-published authors at various stages of their journey, from book creation to marketing.

1. Book Creation Tools

Creating a well-structured, high-quality book requires effective tools that simplify writing, designing, and publishing.

- **Blurb:** Ideal for authors creating both print and eBooks, Blurb offers easy-to-use design tools or the option to upload custom designs. You can publish directly through Blurb or integrate it into broader distribution networks, including Amazon and IngramSpark. Blurb's quality printing and wide range of customization options make it ideal for creating visually appealing books, particularly for authors producing photography books, art collections, or coffee table books.

    o   *Website:* blurb.com

- **Scrivener:** For authors with complex projects, Scrivener is a powerful writing tool that allows you to organize drafts, notes, and research in a single space. It's especially useful for writing novels, screenplays, and academic papers where you need to jump between sections or keep track of intricate details.
    - *Website:* literatureandlatte.com/scrivener
- **Reedsy:** More than just a writing tool, Reedsy provides a comprehensive online editor along with a marketplace where you can find cover designers, editors, and marketing professionals. The platform offers self-published authors access to top industry experts, making it a valuable resource at all stages of the publishing process.
    - *Website:* reedsy.com

2. Editing and Proofreading

A professional edit can dramatically improve the quality and readability of your book. Whether you prefer using editing software or hiring a professional editor, these tools can help ensure your book is polished.

- **ProWritingAid:** This AI-powered grammar and style checker helps authors improve sentence structure, clarity, and readability. In addition to correcting grammar mistakes, it provides insights into pacing, passive voice, and overused words.
    - *Website:* prowritingaid.com
- **Reedsy Marketplace:** For authors looking for human expertise, Reedsy connects you with a wide selection of professional editors. Each editor is vetted for their qualifications, ensuring you'll find experts who specialize in your genre.
    - *Website:* reedsy.com

- **Scribendi:** A fast and professional editing service that helps authors refine their manuscripts. Scribendi offers services ranging from proofreading to in-depth critiques, ensuring that your book is polished and error-free.
  - *Website:* scribendi.com

3. **Cover Design**

Your book's cover is its first impression, and these resources will help you create a design that attracts readers.

- **Canva:** A beginner-friendly tool with customizable templates for DIY book cover designs. Ideal for authors on a budget.
  - *Website:* canva.com
- **99Designs:** A design marketplace where professional designers submit ideas based on your preferences. You choose the design that fits your vision.
  - *Website:* 99designs.com
- **Reedsy Marketplace:** A platform for connecting with experienced cover designers who specialize in publishing, ensuring a polished and professional result.
  - *Website:* reedsy.com

4. **Formatting Tools**

Proper formatting is key to producing a book that looks professional, whether it's in print or digital form.

- **Vellum:** A favorite among Mac users, Vellum simplifies formatting for both eBooks and print books with intuitive design tools and seamless export options.
  - *Website:* vellum.pub
- **Blurb BookWright:** A free tool from Blurb that offers user-friendly options for creating and formatting print

and eBooks. It's particularly suited for visually rich books like photo collections.
- *Website:* blurb.com/bookwright
- **Reedsy Book Editor:** An online tool for writing, editing, and formatting manuscripts. It's free and designed to help self-published authors prepare their books for distribution.
  - *Website:* reedsy.com/write-a-book

5. Distribution Platforms

After formatting, it's time to distribute your book. These platforms offer worldwide reach.

- **Amazon Kindle Direct Publishing (KDP):** The go-to platform for eBook and print-on-demand publishing. KDP offers access to millions of readers through Amazon's marketplace and up to 70 percent royalties.
  - *Website:* kdp.amazon.com
- **IngramSpark:** Provides print-on-demand and wide distribution to bookstores, libraries, and online retailers globally. A good option for authors seeking more control over their print quality and distribution.
  - *Website:* ingramspark.com
- **Blurb:** Beyond its formatting tools, Blurb offers distribution through Amazon, Ingram, and its own platform, allowing authors to reach a wide audience.
  - *Website:* blurb.com/distribution

6. Marketing Tools

Effective marketing strategies are essential for reaching your target audience and ensuring your book's success. The tools below help you promote your book, build an engaged reader base, and manage communications with your audience.

- **Mailchimp:**

  Mailchimp is a popular email marketing platform that allows authors to engage with their readers through regular newsletters, promotional campaigns, and email list management. With tools for designing email templates, tracking performance, and segmenting audiences, Mailchimp helps authors build lasting relationships with their readers. Whether you're promoting a new release, offering special deals, or sending updates about your writing process, Mailchimp provides a comprehensive suite of tools to keep your audience informed and engaged.

  o **Website:** mailchimp.com

- **Kit:**

  Specifically designed for creators, Kit offers a more streamlined experience for authors looking to grow their audience through email marketing. It's built to help authors connect with their readers in a meaningful way, with features like automated email sequences, personalized tagging, and easy-to-create landing pages for book promotions. Kit also integrates with other platforms like WordPress and Shopify, making it a versatile option for managing your marketing funnel from start to finish.

  o **Website:** kit.com

- **StoryOrigin:**

  StoryOrigin is a platform that allows authors to collaborate with other writers for cross-promotions, share advanced reader copies (ARCs), and grow their email lists. It's a valuable tool for building your marketing network while offering readers sneak peeks and special content to increase engagement. StoryOrigin's focus on author collaborations makes it easier to reach new audiences through shared promotions and group giveaways, helping you expand your reader base.

  o **Website:** storyoriginapp.com

7. Cost-Effective Author Website Builders

An author's website acts as the digital hub for their brand, providing a place to showcase books, blog posts, and other projects while connecting with readers. These website builders make it easy to create a professional, functional site without requiring advanced coding skills.

- **WordPress:**

    WordPress is the most widely used website platform, offering nearly endless customization options. With thousands of themes, plugins, and SEO tools, it's perfect for authors who want full control over their website's design and functionality. While WordPress has a steeper learning curve than other site builders, its flexibility makes it ideal for authors looking to grow their site into a powerful marketing tool. Plus, it's well-suited for integrating e-commerce solutions like WooCommerce, making it possible to sell books directly from your site.

    o Website: wordpress.org

- **Squarespace:**

    Known for its sleek, modern templates and user-friendly interface, Squarespace is an excellent option for authors who want a professional website without the complexity of WordPress. It offers built-in e-commerce capabilities, blogging tools, and responsive design, making it easy to create a site that looks great on any device. Squarespace is also known for its excellent customer support, which is helpful for authors new to building websites.

    o Website: squarespace.com

- **Wix:**

    Wix is a beginner-friendly website builder that uses a drag-and-drop interface, allowing authors to easily create and customize their websites. With its wide variety of templates, Wix is a great choice for authors who want to build a functional, visually appealing website without having to code. It also includes features for blogging, social media integration, and basic e-commerce, making it a suitable choice for authors just starting to develop their online presence.

- o   Website: wix.com

8.  **Selling Direct from Your Website**

Selling your books directly from your website gives you more control over the sales process, higher profit margins, and direct access to customer data. The platforms below provide e-commerce solutions for self-published authors to manage sales seamlessly.

- **Shopify:**

    Shopify is a powerful e-commerce platform that allows you to set up an online store and sell products directly to your readers. It's highly customizable and can integrate with your existing website or serve as a stand-alone store. Shopify offers numerous payment gateways, inventory management tools, and marketing integrations, making it easy for authors to handle sales, track orders, and connect with customers. Whether you're selling physical copies, eBooks, or merchandise, Shopify provides a scalable solution for authors looking to monetize their work directly.

    - o   Website: shopify.com

- **WooCommerce:**

    WooCommerce is a free, open-source e-commerce plugin for WordPress, perfect for authors who want to sell both physical and digital books. It's highly customizable, allowing authors to tailor their store to their specific needs. With numerous add-ons for payment gateways, shipping, and digital downloads, WooCommerce integrates seamlessly with a WordPress site, giving authors control over their store's appearance and functionality while leveraging WordPress's powerful SEO features.

- o   Website: woocommerce.com
- **Blurb:**

    In addition to its book creation tools, Blurb offers an online store where authors can sell their books directly. This platform is especially useful for authors of visually rich books, such as photography books or coffee table collections. Blurb's integration with other major retailers like Amazon and IngramSpark ensures that authors can also benefit from wide distribution while maintaining a direct sales channel for higher profits and a closer connection with their readers.

    - o   Website: blurb.com/sell

9.   Analytics and Performance Tracking

Tracking the performance of your marketing efforts and book sales is vital for making informed decisions about your next steps. By understanding where your audience is coming from and how they are interacting with your content, you can optimize your strategies and increase your book's visibility.

- **Google Analytics:**

    Google Analytics is the gold standard for tracking website traffic and understanding visitor behavior. For authors with their own websites, this tool provides deep insights into how visitors find your site, which pages they view, and how long they stay. It also tracks conversions, such as newsletter sign-ups or book purchases, helping you assess the effectiveness of your marketing campaigns. By analyzing this data, you can identify which marketing channels bring the most traffic and adjust your promotional efforts accordingly.

    - o   Website: analytics.google.com

- **Book Report:**

    Specifically designed for Amazon KDP authors, Book Report simplifies the process of tracking book sales and royalties. It provides an easy-to-read dashboard with graphs and data that give you a clear picture of your daily sales, revenue, and trends over time. For authors publishing on Amazon, it's an invaluable tool for monitoring the financial performance of your books without getting bogged down by complex reports.

    o   Website: getbookreport.com

- **Amazon Author Central:**

    Amazon Author Central is a free tool that allows you to manage your author profile and track your book's performance on Amazon. Through Author Central, you can access detailed sales data, track customer reviews, and see where your book is ranking in various categories. Additionally, you can update your biography, upload author photos, and link your blog to help readers learn more about you and your work. It's an essential resource for managing your presence on the world's largest book marketplace.

    o   Website: author.amazon.com

- **Mailchimp Reports:**

    If you use Mailchimp for email marketing, its reporting tools provide detailed insights into your campaigns. You can track email open rates, clicks, and audience engagement over time. This data allows you to refine your messaging and understand which types of content resonate most with your readers, helping you maintain a strong connection with your audience.

    o   Website: mailchimp.com

10. Author Communities and Networking

Building a support network of fellow authors and industry professionals can significantly enhance your self-publishing career. These communities provide opportunities for learning, collaboration, and promotion.

- **Alliance of Independent Authors (ALLi):**

    ALLi is a global nonprofit organization that supports and advocates for self-published authors. By joining ALLi, you gain access to a wealth of resources, including marketing advice, legal guidance, and self-publishing best practices. The community is also a great place to connect with other indie authors, share experiences, and get advice on challenges unique to the self-publishing world. ALLi frequently hosts webinars, offers discounts on publishing services, and provides opportunities to promote your work.

    o   Website: allianceindependentauthors.org

- **Goodreads Author Program:**

    Goodreads is one of the largest social platforms for book lovers, making it an excellent place for authors to engage with readers. Through the Goodreads Author Program, you can claim your author profile, participate in discussions, and interact with readers through book reviews and ratings. Authors can also use Goodreads to host giveaways, helping to generate buzz and increase visibility for new releases. By engaging with the Goodreads community, you can foster a loyal readership and promote your books organically.

    o   Website: goodreads.com/author/program

- **Reedsy Discovery:**

    Reedsy Discovery is a platform designed to help indie authors gain exposure through book reviews from influencers and readers. After submitting your book, Reedsy connects you with reviewers who can help amplify your work within the indie author community. This platform also offers cross-promotion opportunities with other authors, helping you build a broader audience and increase your book's visibility across different reader groups.

    o   Website: reedsy.com/discovery

11. Book Launch and Promotion

A successful book launch is one of the most important phases in the life of your book. It sets the tone for how your book will perform in the market and can drive early sales, reviews, and reader interest. The platforms below can help you manage your launch and get your book in front of the right audience.

- **BookFunnel:**

    BookFunnel is a tool that simplifies the process of delivering digital copies of your book to beta readers, reviewers, or newsletter subscribers. With BookFunnel, you can send eBooks in various formats (ePub, Mobi, PDF) and ensure that readers can easily download your book onto their preferred devices. It's particularly helpful for organizing ARC (Advance Reader Copy) distributions ahead of your book launch, making it easier to gather early reviews and feedback. Additionally, BookFunnel integrates with email marketing platforms, allowing you to grow your mailing list during the launch process.

    o   Website: bookfunnel.com

- **BookBub:**

    BookBub is one of the most powerful platforms for promoting discounted eBooks to a large audience. With millions of dedicated readers subscribed to their daily deals, a feature on BookBub can significantly boost your sales and visibility, particularly if you're offering a limited-time discount. BookBub allows authors to reach new readers by targeting promotions to specific genres and reader preferences. It's especially effective during launch promotions or price drops for established books.

- o **Website:** partners.bookbub.com
- **NetGalley:**

  NetGalley is a platform designed to help authors and publishers distribute review copies to key influencers, including librarians, booksellers, media, and professional reviewers. By submitting your book to NetGalley, you can reach a wide audience of early reviewers who can provide valuable feedback and promote your book through their own channels. NetGalley is particularly useful for generating buzz in the months leading up to your book's release, helping to build momentum and secure important prelaunch reviews.

  - o **Website:** netgalley.com

## 12. Additional Learning Resources

The self-publishing landscape is constantly evolving, with new tools, strategies, and industry changes emerging all the time. To stay competitive and continuously improve your craft, you must keep learning. Below are some of the best resources for self-published authors to stay updated on the latest trends, hone their writing skills, and learn advanced marketing techniques.

- **The Creative Penn Podcast:**

  Hosted by bestselling indie author Joanna Penn, *The Creative Penn Podcast* is a must-listen for anyone serious about self-publishing. Joanna shares insights on everything from writing and publishing strategies to creative entrepreneurship and the future of publishing. The podcast features interviews with industry experts and successful authors, providing actionable advice on self-publishing, book marketing, and more. Whether you're looking to improve your writing or learn about the latest marketing tools, this podcast is an invaluable resource for both new and seasoned authors.

- o   Website: thecreativepenn.com/podcasts
- **Reedsy Learning:**

  Reedsy Learning offers free courses designed to help authors succeed at every stage of the self-publishing journey. These bite-sized email courses cover a wide range of topics, from mastering the writing craft to navigating the complexities of self-publishing. Courses are delivered over a series of days or weeks, making them easy to fit into your schedule. Some of the most popular courses focus on book marketing, editing techniques, and building an author platform. If you're looking to sharpen your skills without spending a fortune, Reedsy Learning is a great place to start.

  - o   Website: reedsy.com/learning
- **Author Marketing Club:**

  Author Marketing Club is a membership-based community offering a wide range of resources and tools to help indie authors succeed. Members gain access to courses on topics like book marketing, self-publishing best practices, and advanced promotional strategies. The club also provides tools to help authors manage their book launches, connect with readers, and generate more sales. With a supportive community and resources tailored to indie authors, Author Marketing Club is an excellent platform for those looking to take their self-publishing efforts to the next level.

  - o   Website: authormarketing.club/

This appendix provides a comprehensive list of essential tools and resources that can help self-published authors navigate every stage of the publishing process—from writing and editing to marketing and sales. Each platform offers unique benefits tailored to different aspects of the self-publishing journey. Whether you're just starting out or looking to optimize your existing process, these resources can significantly improve your chances of success. Be sure to explore the options that align with your goals and continuously adapt to the changing publishing landscape to stay ahead of the curve.

# REFERENCES

"About IU," Indies Unlimited, December 21, 2023, https://indiesunlimited.com/about/.

"About the CIP Program," Library of Congress, n.d., https://www.loc.gov/programs/cataloging-in-publication/about-this-program/.

"About us," Hometown Reads," n.d., http://www.hometownreads.com/about/.

"Book Review Submission Service," Feathered Quill, December 3, 2024, https://featheredquill.com/.

"Book Reviews and Coverage of Indie Publishers," Foreword Reviews, n.d., https://www.forewordreviews.com/.

"Build an audience with a professional book review," BlueInk Review, n.d., https://www.blueinkreview.com/.

"Corporate Email Signature Generator," Newoldstamp, October 13, 2024, https://newoldstamp.com/.

"Create an Alert - Google Search Help," Google, n.d., https://support.google.com/websearch/answer/4815696?hl=en.

"Create Videos Online in Minutes. Social Video Marketing Made Easy. A Video Maker That Turns Text Into Video Marketing Content in Minutes," Lumen5, n.d., https://lumen5.com/.

"Discover and recommend books," NetGalley, n.d., https://www.netgalley.com/.

"Discover Books," Kirkus Reviews, n.d., https://www.kirkusreviews.com/book-lists/.

Dube, Monica, "The ARC Review Process: Build Your ARC Team and Get Reviews," PublishDrive, August 20, 2024, https://publishdrive.com/how-to-get-book-reviews-and-build-an-arc-team.html. "Financial Infrastructure to Grow Your Revenue," Stripe, n.d., https://stripe.com/.

"Find the Best Global Talent," Fiverr, n.d., https://www.fiverr.com/hire/web-design.

"Forget cookie-cutter ecommerce," WooCommerce, December 5, 2024, https://woocommerce.com/.

"Free and Customizable Book Templates," Canva, n.d., https://www.canva.com/templates/s/book/.

"FREE & Discount eBooks," Choosy Bookworm, n.d., https://choosybookworm.com/.

"Free PR leads to build media connections that make a difference," PitchRate, n.d., https://pitchrate.com.

"Free Online Video Maker," Animoto, n.d., https://animoto.com/.

Gatson, Starla, "Creative Ways to Grow Your Email List," Constant Contact, June 24, 2024, https://www.constantcontact.com/blog/grow-email-list/.

"Get Amazing Deals on Bestselling EBooks," BookBub, n.d., https://www.bookbub.com/.

"Get Honest Book Reviews on Amazon," BookSirens, n.d., https://booksirens.com/.

Hamilton, Jason, "How to Create a WordPress Website for Authors in 7 Easy Steps," Kindlepreneur, December 20, 2023, https://kindlepreneur.com/wordpress-website-for-authors/.

"Home page," BookLife, n.d., https://booklife.com.

"How Do I Create a Goodreads Account?," Goodreads, n.d., https://help.goodreads.com/s/article/How-do-I-create-a-Goodreads-account "Pay Friends Payments App," Venmo, n.d., https://venmo.com/.

"Marketing, Automation & Amp; Email Platform," Mailchimp, n.d., https://mailchimp.com/?currency=EUR.

# REFERENCES

"MDS: 006," LibraryThing, n.d., https://www.librarything.com/mds/006.

"Medium: Read and Write Stories," Medium, n.d., https://medium.com/.

"Online Press Release Distribution Service," PRWeb, n.d., https://www.prweb.com/.

"Online Printing Services," VistaPrint, n.d., https://www.vistaprint.com/?srsltid=AfmBOoqJD84ig6eE4RHGUV-hRQEZl5FU-EsSA7QaUWGALk5GizUXhsj0.

"Payflow Payment Gateway Service," PayPal, n.d., https://www.paypal.com/us/webapps/mpp/payflow-payment-gateway.

"Payment Platform - In-Person & Online Payment Gateway," Square," n.d., https://squareup.com/us/en/payments/payment-platform.

"Press Release Distribution and Press Release Service," PressRelease.com, n.d., https://www.pressrelease.com/.

"Product Overview," MatchMaker.fm, n.d., https://www.matchmaker.fm/.

Schmidt, Kathleen, "Do Trade Reviews Still Matter?" *Publishing Confidential* (blog), October 18, 2023, https://kathleenschmidt.substack.com/p/do-trade-reviews-still-matter.

"Tell your story: suddenly, connected," Qwoted, n.d., https://www.qwoted.com.

"The Best Web Hosting," Bluehost, n.d., https://www.bluehost.com/cs/special/wordpress-campaigns1.

"The easiest way to create professional ads and social media images for your books," Book Brush, n.d., https://bookbrush.com/.

"The media wants your stories and this is where they look," SourceBottle, n.d., https://www.sourcebottle.com/.

"The ultimate speaker toolbox," SpeakerTunity, n.d., https://www.speakertunity.com/.

"Turn Your Browser Into a Marketer's Best Friend," Keywords Everywhere, n.d., https://keywordseverywhere.com/.

"Want to Get FREE Publicity for Your Books? Try Pitch Rate," Book Pleasures, n.d., https://www.bookpleasures.com/websitepublisher/articles/1131/1/Want-to-Get-FREE-Publicity-for-Your-Books-Try-Pitch-Rate/Page1.html.

"Web Hosting Perfected – SiteGround," SiteGround, n.d., https://world.siteground.com/.

"Welcome to your place on the net to find your next favorite book," My Book Place, n.d., https://mybookplace.net/.

"What Do Effective Book Marketing Campaigns Accomplish?" Smith Publicity, November 13, 2024, https://www.smithpublicity.com/.

"Where Awesome Book Readers Meet Awesome Writers," Awesome Gang, n.d., https://awesomegang.com/.

"WiseStamp - Generate & Manage Professional Email Signatures," WiseStamp, November 13, 2024, https://www.wisestamp.com/.

"Wix Website Builder," Wix, n.d., https://www.wix.com.

Zalani, Rochi, "Hootsuite Vs. Buffer: Which Social Media Management Tool Is Right for You?," August 5, 2024, https://zapier.com/blog/hootsuite-vs-buffer/.

# YOUR FEEDBACK MEANS THE WORLD TO ME

Thank you for taking the time to read my book. Your support and feedback are invaluable in helping me create better books and share my knowledge with more authors like you. Your review doesn't just help me—it helps other authors decide if this book can help them too.

If you found this book helpful, I would be deeply grateful if you could take just sixty seconds to leave an honest review on Amazon (or the platform where you purchased the book).

Your review doesn't have to be long—just a star rating and a few sentences about your thoughts, what other readers could use to determine whether this is the book for them, or how the book helped you would be wonderful. Reviews not only guide future readers but also help me continue improving and reaching more people.

**Here's how to leave a review:**

1. Visit the book's page on Amazon (or your preferred retailer).
2. Scroll to the "Leave a Review" section.
3. Select your star rating and write a few words about your experience.

That's it! Your feedback is a gift, and I truly appreciate your time and effort in sharing it.

Thank you for being part of this journey and for your incredible support. I hope this book brought a fresh outlook and a new direction to assist in your marketing goals!

# ABOUT THE AUTHOR

Dr. Stephanie Krol's journey encompasses a wealth of knowledge and diverse experiences in education, real estate, publishing, and digital marketing. With a Doctorate in education, she has served as the past Dean of Schools in Higher Education for For-profit Allied Health Schools, a Professor, a Training and Development Manager, a curriculum writer, and a nonprofit membership specialist for a couple counties. She currently co-owns a Real Estate School, Real Estate Referral Brokerage, and Publishing Services and Digital Marketing companies.

Her proudest achievements are the success of her dog's health journey, the multi-award-winning book that came out of it for other people to heal their pets, and her previous competitive horseback riding. She empowers dog owners with unique, commonsense approaches to health and wellness, species-appropriate feeding, and research-backed nutrition plans that enhance their pets' vitality and well-being, preventing disease and pain for your furry family friends.

Publications:

- *What the Pet Food Industry Is Not Telling You: Developing Good Practices for a Healthier Dog*: This award-winning book has garnered eleven national awards, one international award, and one global award in 2024, establishing Dr. Krol as a leading voice in pet health, wellness, and nutrition.
- *Illinois Real Estate License Law and Principles*: A Simplified Explanation of the Essential Knowledge Every Licensee Needs to Know to Pass the State Real Estate License Exam. This book reflects Dr. Krol's expertise as an educator and over twenty years of real estate knowledge, along with her co-author and her deep commitment to the real estate profession, specifically in the state of Illinois, where her real estate school resides.
- *Commonsense and Outcome-Driven Marketing for Authors*: Drawing on her experience as a digital marketing strategist and owner of a full-service agency for both large and small businesses, this practical guide equips self-published authors with strategies to effectively market their books and achieve their unique goals.
- Additional books are coming forth in Digital Marketing for Small and Large Businesses, Digital Marketing for Real Estate Brokerages, and a novel.

Credentials and Achievements:

- **Degrees:** Doctorate in education, master's in organizational leadership and public administration, and a bachelor's in psychology (with minors in applied English and communication).
- **Certifications and Licenses:** Certified Functional Medicine Practitioner, Certified Health and Well-being Coach, Certified Raw Dog Nutrition Specialist, Certified Raw Dog Nutrition Specialist and Dog Health Coach, Certifications in Animal Behavior for Dogs, Cats, and

## ABOUT THE AUTHOR

Rabbits, Certified through the American Association of Drugless Practitioners (AADP), Certified Publishing Consultant, and Licensed Broker in Michigan for over twenty years and Illinois for over ten years.

- **Professional Affiliations:** International Association of Canine Professionals (Professional Status and Member), Nonfiction Authors Association, Midwest Independent Publishers Association, Independent Book Publishers Association, Alliance for Independent Authors Author's Guild, and the Marquis Who Who's Publications Board.

Dr. Krol is a multi-award-winning national and internationally published author who operates her own imprint and hybrid company and offers comprehensive publishing services for self-published authors worldwide. She supports authors across all genres in self-publishing, hybrid publishing, and various formats, including paperbacks, hardcovers, eBooks, and audiobooks.

Through her work, Dr. Krol advocates for health and wellness for both people and their pets while nurturing the success of authors worldwide.

# INVITE DR. STEPHANIE TO SPEAK AT YOUR NEXT EVENT

If you found value in this book and are planning a summit, training, or live event, I'd love to contribute as a speaker for this topic or others.

From author marketing to performance-driven education reform, I bring practical strategies, dynamic energy, and decades of experience that equip audiences to take immediate action.

Scan the QR code on this page or visit my speaking page to learn more. You can also schedule time directly through the website. I look forward to connecting and contributing to your event's success!

www.ingramcontent.com/pod-product-compliance
Lightning Source LLC
Chambersburg PA
CBHW071958070526
44583CB00015B/1249